34/4

THE DECORATIVE ARTS
OF AFRICA

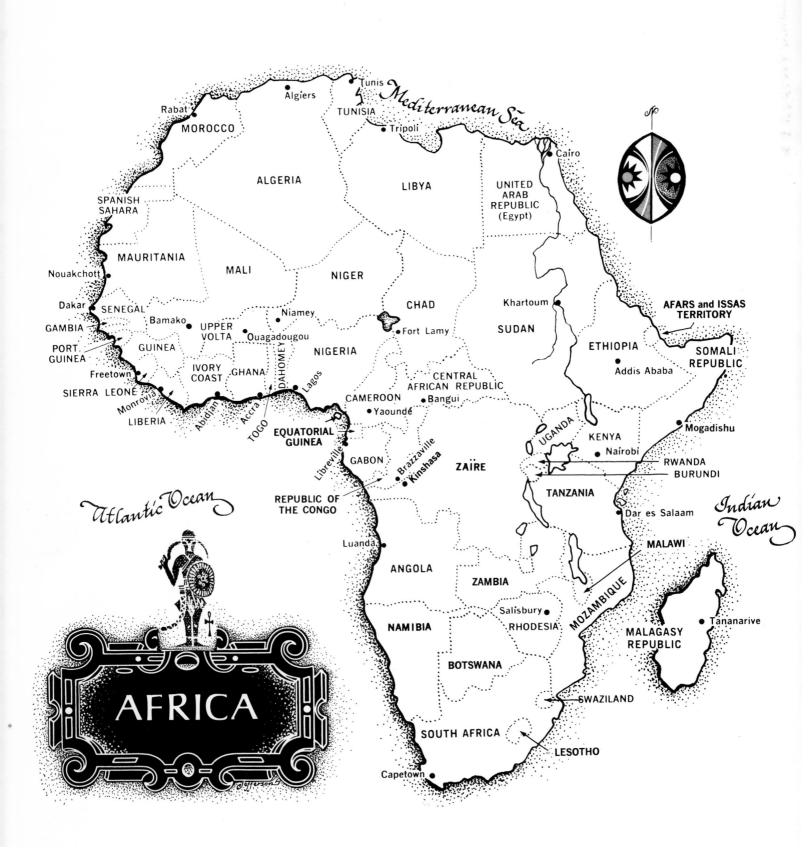

Rabat
Algiers
Tunis
MOROCCO
TUNISIA
Tripoli
Mediterranean Sea
Cairo
SPANISH
SAHARA
ALGERIA
LIBYA
UNITED
ARAB
REPUBLIC
(Egypt)
MAURITANIA
MALI
NIGER
CHAD
Khartoum
Nouakchott
AFARS and ISSAS
TERRITORY
Dakar
SENEGAL
Niamey
Fort Lamy
SUDAN
ETHIOPIA
SOMALI
REPUBLIC
GAMBIA
Bamako
UPPER
VOLTA
Ouagadougou
Addis Ababa
PORT.
GUINEA
GUINEA
NIGERIA
Lagos
CENTRAL
AFRICAN REPUBLIC
Freetown
IVORY
COAST
GHANA
DAHOMEY
SIERRA LEONE
Monrovia
Abidjan
Accra
TOGO
CAMEROON
Bangui
Mogadishu
LIBERIA
Yaoundé
EQUATORIAL
GUINEA
UGANDA
KENYA
Libreville
GABON
Brazzaville
Kinshasa
ZAÏRE
Nairobi
RWANDA
BURUNDI
REPUBLIC OF
THE CONGO
TANZANIA
Atlantic Ocean
Dar es Salaam
Indian
Ocean
Luanda
MALAWI
ANGOLA
ZAMBIA
MOZAMBIQUE
Salisbury
NAMIBIA
RHODESIA
MALAGASY
REPUBLIC
Tananarive
BOTSWANA
SWAZILAND
SOUTH AFRICA
LESOTHO
Capetown

AFRICA

THE DECORATIVE ARTS OF AFRICA

Louise E. Jefferson

Collins   St. James's Place   London, 1974

ACKNOWLEDGMENTS

I wish to thank those whose early interest and assistance were encouraging: Hazel V. Orton, Nina Millen, Allan Ranck, Margaret Shannon, Frederick Patterson, Ella Griffin, Pauli Murray, and Constance Stone.

I am deeply grateful to Morris Colman, without whose constant guidance and foresight this book might not have been attempted.

I owe very special thanks to a patient and efficient editor, Barbara Burn of The Viking Press, and to Barbara Tyrrell of Natal, South Africa, Barbara Rubin of UCLA, Margaret Webster Plass of the University Museum in Philadelphia, Mrs. Manteau of the French Embassy in Washington, D.C., and Cyrus Leroy Baldridge of Santa Fe.

For substantial support in the projection of this book, I am indebted to The Ford Foundation. Thanks are also due to the following institutions and organizations for their help: The Metropolitan Museum of Art; The Cooper-Hewitt Museum of Decorative Arts and Design; The Smithsonian Institution; The United Nations; The American Museum of Natural History; Harvard University Press; the Musée Royal de l'Afrique Centrale in Tervuren; the Ghana Museums and Monuments Board; the Tanzania Ministry of Information; the embassies of Tunisia and Morocco; A. Brunnschweiler of Manchester, England; The Ghana Universities Press; *Nigeria* Magazine; Dover Publications; National Development Corporation of Dar es Salaam; Books of Africa in Johannesburg; The Schomburg Collection of the New York Public Library; the South African Tourist Corporation; *African Arts Magazine*; the editors of *Man*, *Expedition* Magazine; the Department of Antiquities, Nigeria; and the Folk Textile Collection in Oxford, England.

For their kindness and interest, I wish to thank Roy Wilkens, Jean Hutson, Dr. Paul Bohannan, Michelle Broster, Louis J. Cowan, Olyve J. Haynes, Joe Nash, Jerry Shane, Professor Robert F. Thompson, Frank M. Snowden, Jr., Dr. William Bascom, Dr. Frank Willett, Florence Johns, Heinz E. Kiewe, Professor Roy Sieber, Richard Ahlborn, Mrs. H. Geluwe, Milton Sonday, Ann Willis, Shirley Anderson, Gertrude Robinson, Lois Jones, Roger Wilkins, Martin Hamer, Carroll Greene, Mel Williamson, Elizabeth Wheeler, Ron Hobbs, Joyce Johnson, Anne Fredericks.

Thanks to my wonderful friends in Africa: Bob Fleming, Bill Sutherland, Omaru Shabaz, Ahmed Aribi, Jerreh Sagnia, Ben Enwonwu, Professor Todd, Afewerk Tekle, Father Kevin Carroll, Sarale Owens, Dr. R. Pankhurst, Oscar Rampone, Elimo Njau, Amye Sanga, Susie Umphrey, Nina Gwatkin, David Heathcote, Claire Simpson, Ekpo Eyo, Martha Buiengo and the Hon. Lady Marian Chesham.

William Collins Sons & Co Ltd
London • Glasgow • Sydney • Auckland • Toronto • Johannesburg

First published in Great Britain in 1974

ISBN: 0 00 216151-6

Printed in U.S.A.

AFRICA'S
MAJOR ETHNIC GROUPS

FRENCH COLS

BERBERS

ARABS

BEDOUINS

ARABS

HAMITES

MOORS

TUAREGS

NUBIANS

ETHIOPIANS

SENEGALESE

HAUSA

YORUBA

ASHANTI IBO

BALUBA PYGMY

KIKUYU

WATUTSI LUO

BAHUTU MASAI

BAKONGO

BUSHMEN BANTU

MALAGASY

AFRIKANER

CAPE COLORED

1. MOROCCO
2. ALGERIA
3. TUNISIA
4. LIBYA
5. U.A.R. EGYPT
6. SPANISH SAHARA
7. IFNI
8. MAURITANIA
9. MALI
10. NIGER
11. CHAD
12. SUDAN
13. ETHIOPIA
14. FR. SOMALILAND
15. SENEGAL
16. GAMBIA
17. PORT. GUINEA
18. GUINEA
19. UPPER VOLTA
20. SIERRA LEONE
21. LIBERIA
22. IVORY COAST
23. GHANA
24. TOGO
25. NIGERIA

26. DAHOMEY
27. CAMEROON
28. CENT. AFRICAN REP.
29. RIO MUNI
30. GABON
31. CONGO-BRAZZAVILLE
32. ZAÏRE
33. UGANDA
34. RWANDA
35. BURUNDI
36. KENYA
37. SOMALIA
38. TANZANIA
39. MALAWI
40. ZAMBIA
40A. RHODESIA
41. MOZAMBIQUE
42. ANGOLA
43. NAMIBIA
44. BOTSWANA
45. SOUTH AFRICA
46. SWAZILAND
47. LESOTHO
48. MALAGASY

Dedicated to

Dr. James H. Robinson

whose *Crossroads Africa* program

has inspired young people

throughout the world

African peoples followed their own road in the past; there is nothing to say that they will not follow it, constructively, creatively, again. Their failings have been common talk for years, for centuries. Now it may be time to speak of their achievements. And their achievements, while the fuller canvas of their history unrolls across these years, will increasingly be seen and understood. We are only at the beginning of that story.

—Basil Davidson, *The Lost Cities of Africa*

CONTENTS

PREFACE

Man's inclination to decorate objects is deep-rooted and universal. Since prehistoric times he has embellished a wide variety of his possessions—from his weapons and the walls of his shelter to clothing and even his own body. Much of what we now consider fine craftsmanship resulted from the simple urge to improve the appearance of things, to achieve designs pleasing to the eye, to enrich both utilitarian and religious objects with familiar patterns and symbols meaningful to the artist and his people.

In recent years, the world has come to recognize and appreciate the beauty and diversity of Africa's art forms, not only for their historical and cultural significance but also for the continuing aesthetic pleasure they afford. Though many people are familiar with the beautiful sculptured figures and masks brought from Africa to Europe by early travelers, the African artist did not express himself only in these forms. For centuries he has produced skillfully fashioned objects in gold, bronze, ivory, and leather; he has also shown his proficiency in the arts of weaving, textile design, basketry, and pottery. Many of the designs, motifs, patterns, and symbols recognized as African are known to date back to the most remote epochs of human time. Hundreds of Stone Age artifacts—axes, spears, arrowheads, and similar weapons—have been discovered in every part of the African continent, including what is now the vast, barren Sahara. Moreover, thousands of paintings and engravings have been found on rock surfaces, and many kinds of implements made of stone, ivory, and bone testify to the skill of gifted Africans who were among the earliest artists in the world.

Adequate coverage of the arts of Africa would require many volumes exploring different branches of learning—history, archaeology, anthropology, folklore, and ethnology. This book, however, is intended only as a visual sampling of what the spirit and tempo of the artist's role has been in the past and what it continues to be today. As Africa enters the mainstream of world developments, exerting its influence on the course of international events, a growing awareness has developed of Africa's cultural past, thanks to the extensive research of dedicated scholars throughout the world. With this new respect for and understanding of traditional art forms, the African artist of today is busy embracing new techniques and ideas, employing new materials, and creating new markets for his work. An example of this industry is Tanzania's production of the lovely printed Khanga and Vitenge cloths to satisfy the ever-increasing tourists. Also intriguing to the traveler are the beautiful woven materials of Senegal and Nigeria, the skillfully designed jewelry of Ethiopia, and the carefully wrought pottery and basketry of Uganda.

As Calvin Douglas of the Brooklyn Museum of Art has pointed out, "Artistic expression is not the luxury to African peoples that it has become to western man. It is considered a natural and necessary way of giving meaning to phases of a person's life and enhancing his work. This tradition continues in independent African countries today, where masks and dance routines are used in political festivals and high officials in many governments remain poets or musicians. If the vitality of a culture can be measured in terms of its ability to produce art and enlarge its conception of human life, it is not difficult to understand why so many black people in the United States today look to Africa as their cultural source." *

In this introduction to the decorative arts of Africa, I have tried to emphasize the richness and diversity of the work rather than to catalogue particular styles by region, tribe, or historical development. Thus, I have divided the book into sections devoted to kinds of work—costume, fabrics, metalwork, wood carving, bead design, and so on—with examples drawn from all over the continent and from different periods of time. I have made no attempt to be all-inclusive by illustrating every kind of work produced by each region, choosing instead to picture the finest examples I could find without regard for political or anthropological divisions. My purpose has been to show the general reader and the interested student the excellence and variety of African craftsmanship as it has manifested itself in the past and as it continues to enrich our lives today.

Louise E. Jefferson
New York, 1972

---

* Calvin Douglas, *African Art,* the Brooklyn Museum of Art, New York, 1969.

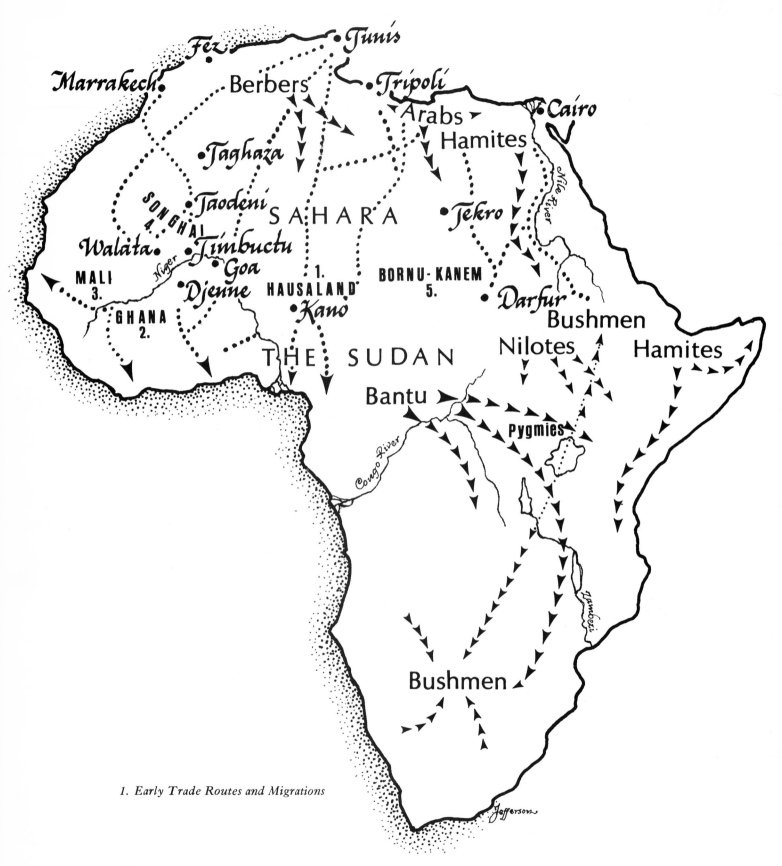

1. Early Trade Routes and Migrations

Marrakech
Fez
Tunis
Berbers
Tripoli
Cairo
Arabs
Hamites
Taghaza
SAHARA
Taodeni
SONGHAI 4.
Tekro
Walata
Timbuctu
Niger
Goa
1.
BORNU-KANEM 5.
Nile River
MALI 3.
HAUSALAND
Djenne
Kano
Darfur
GHANA 2.
Bushmen
THE SUDAN
Nilotes
Hamites
Bantu
Pygmies
Congo River
Zambezi
Bushmen
Jefferson

INTRODUCTION

The Beginnings

The immense variety of the arts of Africa may perhaps be explained in part by the great variety offered by the continent itself. The African land is huge, and the dark races of predominantly Negro strain are scattered over vast areas separated by wide savannas, burning deserts, dense rain forests, lofty mountains, and turbulent rivers. At one time the Sahara Desert was a fertile land and the site of Africa's first works or art, the rock paintings of perhaps ten thousand years ago; but, as the glaciers moved north from Europe, the lakes and rivers of the Sudan dried up, and life moved south (fig. 1).

Although the great desert has for millennia been a barrier between north and south Africa, effectively cutting off communication except through occasional caravans of traders, explorers, and nomads, the problem of cultural origins in sub-Saharan Africa has remained a source of much controversy. As Europeans from the fifteenth century on discovered the advanced civilizations of Africa, they found it difficult to believe that these cultures had not somehow been touched by influences from outside Africa. Dr. Frank Willett, in discussing the early cave paintings, says, "Many allegedly foreign influences have been claimed in the art. The Abbé Breuil in particular interpreted some subjects as Sumerian or Egyptian, but none of these suggestions can be substantiated." *

Yet, the question of Egyptian influence is not easily dismissed. Dr. David O'Connor asks, "Was there any serious contact between ancient Egypt and black Africa, that is the Negroid and Negro peoples of western and central Africa; and, if there was, how important was the flow of influences in either direction? This is not just an academic question, for many Africans and Afro-Americans, intensely interested in the history of early African cultures, often feel that the creativity of these cultures has been unfairly minimized by European scholarship. This is not true of historians and prehistorians of Africa today; the old habit of attributing any unusually sophisticated idea or technique appearing amongst black Africans to the influence or the presence of a racially 'superior' Hamite or other non-Negro has rightly been abandoned." ** Nevertheless, he recognizes that many ancient peoples, including the Greeks, borrowed from Egyptian civilization, and that it cannot be determined to what extent similarities in Egyptian and black African art can be explained by cultural interchange and what ascribed to a general African nature (fig. 2).

* Frank Willett, *African Art*, New York, 1971.
** David O'Connor, *Expedition*, vol. 14, no. 1, Philadelphia, 1971.

The rock pictures in the Atlas Mountains and in various parts of the Sahara were first investigated by Leo Frobenius in 1913. It is believed by most scientists today that what are now dry regions of scorching sands were once fertile plains where herds of cattle grazed. Much of the ecology of the Sahara during prehistoric times can be determined by the subject matter portrayed in the rock pictures. There were long-horned buffalo (*bubalus antiquus*, now extinct), elephants, oxen, sheep, and other animals that cannot survive in this area today. The human figures pictured are generally hunters with bows and arrows, javelins, and short swords. These portraits show remarkable care in their delineation and give us much information about early crafts and decorative arts. The Stone Age men of the Sahara region were familiar with pictorial motifs as a result of working decorations into their weapons and tools. Using the same techniques, they chiseled their stories and designs into the rocks and decorated them with color. Mineral pigments were used, the most common colors being red, brown, green, yellow, and shades of blue. Many of the human figures have light skin and hair (fig. 3), and in some the hair is arranged in a chignon piled high on the forehead, a style still used among the Peul and Fulbe women who live on the upper reaches of the Niger and Senegal Rivers today.

Rock paintings can be found all over Africa, not just in the northern regions (fig. 4); in fact, the painted caves in parts of South Africa offer as much information about the early inhabitants of those areas as do the clay tablets of Mesopotamia and the stone slabs of Egypt. Probably the most discussed painting of southern Africa is the "white lady" of Brandberg (fig. 5), which makes an interesting contrast with the Algerian "white lady" above. Because of what we know about the Africans' use of white body decoration, this painting is sometimes thought to indicate the mysterious appearance of a white woman among the native Africans. Henri Lhote and Abbé Breuil, among others, describe these paintings in great detail and offer much speculation about their significance.

The earliest known inhabitants of South Africa were the Bushmen, who lived in the rocky outcroppings of the Namib Desert, an area now known as Namibia. They decorated the flat

2. Drawing after a fourteenth-century wall painting in the tomb of Hoy, Viceregent of Nubia (original in Neues Museum, Berlin)

12

3. The "White Lady" of Auanrhet, Tassili (Algeria), c. 5000–1200 B.C.

rock surfaces of that region with some of the finest rock paintings in the world, portraying fierce battles with the Bantu from the north and the Boer settlers from the south, and showing various kinds of wild animals and plants on which their livelihood depended. Recent interpretations of the pictures have been made in light of Bushman legends, and symbolic meanings have been assigned to certain animals depicted; earlier assumptions that these pictures were simply a form of hunting magic have been dismissed for the most part, since some favorite quarries, such as the eland and springbok, rarely appear.

Greatly outnumbered by their enemies, many Bushmen were killed, while others retreated to remote spots in the hills. Today, as before, they live as nomads, hunting wild animals and gathering wild foods. They roam in almost constant search for water, which they carry in what is probably their only decorated implement today (fig. 6).

One of the most beautiful Bushman paintings shows a flock of ostriches of various colors and a close look reveals that one of the birds has human legs, and that a bow and arrow is hidden in the feathers; obviously a Bushman has disguised himself as an ostrich in order to get close to the flock. The general character of Bushman art is naturalistic, showing a fine observation of contour and perspective. In some cases the pictures are painted in fine colors; in others they are chipped into the rock. Stone slabs and mortars for grinding colors have been found in several of the caves. The pulverized mineral pigments were apparently mixed with fat to provide the proper viscosity, and very thin and pliable bone points were used to achieve fine lines, which are drawn with admirable precision.

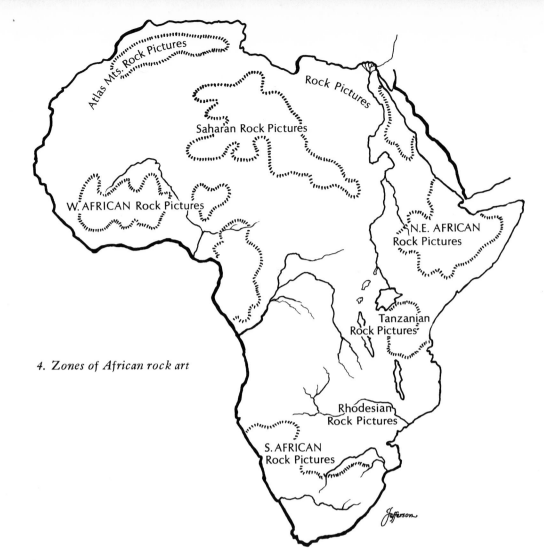

4. *Zones of African rock art*

5. Left: *The "White Lady" of Brandberg, Tsisab Gorge (South Africa)*

6. Below: *Bushman engraving on ostrich shell used for carrying water (Namibia, South Africa)*

7. *Bushman painting of landscape and hunters (Botswana, South Africa)*

8. *Bushman cave painting (Southwest Africa)*

The African Craftsman

As we have seen, the African artist has been a prominent member of his community since prehistoric times, not only as a creator of the magnificent rock pictures but also as the fashioner of decorated implements for hunting and other everyday activities. Throughout the invasions, explorations, trading systems, and cultural exchanges occurring after 1000 B.C., the African arts flourished. With the migrations and the settling of various tribes in new regions, the regional craftsmen, clinging to some of their ancient traditions, became known for their styles of workmanship; jewelry, weaving, carving, and pottery continued to carry the style of the group to which the craftsman belonged.

The African artist and craftsman today still holds a respected position within his group, though his social status is not the same everywhere. There is often a sharp dividing line between the crafts practiced by men and those practiced by women. In most regions, men are responsible for house-building, tool-making, and carving, while the women are adept at dyeing, spinning, making pottery, and weaving. In many parts of west Africa, however, men do the weaving and even the fashioning of garments.

Professional techniques are usually learned and handed down from father to son, and certain crafts are often a family enterprise. In some cases, however, when a young member of the tribe shows talent at carving, for instance, he may serve an apprenticeship with a well-known sculptor, paying his teacher with gifts provided by his family. If his skill comes to the attention of the village chief, the artist is ordered to help create the elaborate attributes of chiefdom: thrones, crowns, scepters, drums, and especially articles of personal adornment. The chief also controls and assigns the commissions of other crafts, such as casting metals and polishing beads. Since the village artists live solely by their chief's patronage, their talents and ideas must conform to his wishes; this explains why the objects created during certain periods in a single village will bear a strong resemblance to one another.

9. *Swazi craftsman (Swaziland, South Africa)*

10. *Basuto woman making pottery (Basutoland, South Africa)*

11. *A weaver from the Ivory Coast*

12. *Men sewing male garments in the marketplace at Bamako (Mali)*

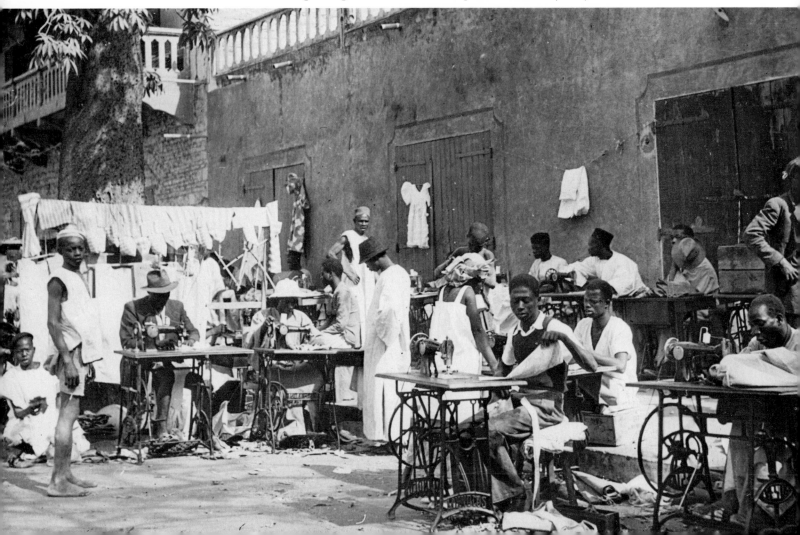

13. Lozi craftsman (Rhodesia)
14. Man making statuettes (Upper Volta)

I. SYMBOLS, PATTERNS, AND MOTIFS

Many of the everyday objects created by the African craftsman are beautifully decorated with intricate designs and patterns, most of which are indigenous to certain parts of the continent. Only a few historians, anthropologists, and collectors have explored the meanings or the importance of the various symbolic designs and devices. It is generally known, however, that the thinking of most African groups is greatly influenced by the many legends, myths, and proverbs of their tribal past, and that these influences are to be noted in much of their art.

Craftsmen often created representational pictures to record time-honored stories and legends, and these designs, arranged in different schemes, eventually became motifs that could be read almost as written texts. These story-teller craftsmen, in accord with tribal traditional, were most interested in the glories of their ancestors and their kings, so that many carvings, castings, and appliquéd patterns depict battles, conquests, and ceremonies involving historical events.

Other patterns originated as simple representations of ordinary tribal activities, such as hunting. Moreover, the African artist, always in constant touch with the elements of his natural environment, has used animals and plants as symbols to represent deities and spirits, or to serve as emblems.

These symbols and motifs have retained their importance throughout the years, some of them changing somewhat through the intermingling of cultures or through gradual stylization, which has led from naturalistic representation to near abstraction. This is not to say that all African patterns have symbolic meanings; some geometrical patterns merely follow the texture of the medium in order to have controlled continuity of design across the area of decoration, while other patterns are made to be enjoyed for their own sake.

EGYPTIAN MOTIFS

In the rock paintings we have seen evidence of sophisticated cultures in Africa long before the time of the Pharaohs, and there is reason to believe that Egyptian civilization owes as much to influences from what is now sub-Saharan Africa as it does to the great cultures of Mesopotamia. Nubia, the "Land of the Blacks," was a source of much of Egypt's wealth, not only in gold but also in men and in cultural traditions. After the fall of the Egyptian kingdom, many of its people fled—some to the east, some to the west along the edge of the desert, and others to the south, to found new kingdoms in the heart of Africa, taking with them familiar patterns and motifs which later became incorporated into their own designs. Many of the Egyptian motifs illustrated here (figs. 15 and 16) are simple geometric patterns; others are stylizations of previously representational narratives; and still others were distinctly intended as symbols of forces or figures important in Egyptian culture.

ARABIC CALLIGRAPHY

When the Moslem religion spread across the Sahara during the seventh century, as Arab armies sought new lands to conquer, some of the great black kingdoms in the south were several

1. Sistrum of Isis
   (conscience)

2. Tet of Osiris
   (stability)

3. Rising Sun of Osiris
   (birth)

4. Sma (union)

5. Buckle of Isis

6. Vulture (funerary sign)

7. Sundial (life)

8. Winged serpent
   (evil)

9. Falcon
   (sun)

10. Phoenix
    (immortality)

11. Pyramid
    (heavenly fire)

12. Scarab
    (longevity)

13. Ankh
    (life)

15. Egyptian symbols

16. Egyptian motifs

centuries old. Many traders from the north were already peacefully settled among the peoples of the upper Niger River, where migrating Moors, Arabs, and Egyptians had merged their traditions with the kingdoms of Ghana, Mali, Bornu, and Songhai. Though the Arabs failed to conquer the Sudanese areas, they did manage to establish contact between the Moslem and Negro worlds, and with the trans-Saharan trade of gold, slaves, salt, cloth, swords, and books came new ideas, including the flowing patterns and intricate geometric designs of Arabic calligraphy (fig. 17).

Since the Moslem religion forbids depiction of human and animal forms, calligraphy has become an important decorative element in Arabic art, and the calligrapher has held a position above that of other artists. Although spoken Arabic may vary from country to country, the calligraphy is understood universally, and its forms appear throughout Africa where the Moslems have made their influence felt. "Used as surface decoration . . . abstracted vegetal and geometric forms, woven into unending patterns of infinite variation, appear not only in architecture, but in the decorative arts—ceramics, metalwork, woodwork, glass, and textiles." *

AFRICAN PATTERNS

Certain fundamental geometric designs are used all over the world, and it is possible, by multiplication, subdivision, and interlacement, to produce an endless variety of shapes. Illustrated in figure 19 are several of these shapes, all of which appear at one point or another in the vast repertory of African designs. Also illustrated are certain African patterns from two different regions, as well as favorite animal motifs drawn from all over the continent. In the chapters that follow we will see hundreds of other similar patterns as they are used in the wide range of African craftsmanship.

* Marie G. Lukens, *Islamic Art*, The Metropolitan Museum of Art, New York, 1965.

1. Seventeenth-century proverb, Bismillah style

2. Koranic verse in the shape of a pear. The leaves and lines below read: "Beauty is the joy of hearts, the balm of injury, the adornment of life and its elixir."

3. Thuluth-style script was the signature of ancient kings.

4. Nineteenth-century double script reads: "Say, each man is his own example; your God knows who of you walks most straight on the path of righteousness."

5. Kufic-style script reads: "Three things enforce rule, mercy, justice, and goodness."

17. Arabic calligraphy

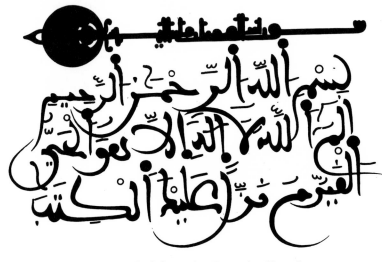

6. A leaf from the Koran in fifteenth-century North African script.

18. Typical Moslem designs used for decorating small objects such as buckles, eyelets, clasps, locks, headbands

25

19. Geometric forms found in African art have been used by
many cultures—Egyptian, Grecian, Roman, Arabian, and Japanese

1. Hausa	*2.* Zaïre (Congo)	*3.* Nigeria	*4.* Zaïre (Congo)	*5.* Egypt
6. Zaïre (Congo)	*7.* Egypt	*8.* Zaïre (Congo)	*9.* Central Africa	*10.* Tunisia
11. Ivory Coast	*12.* Zaïre (Congo)	*13.* Chad	*14.* Angola	*15.* Tunisia
16. Cameroon	*17.* Zaïre (Congo)	*18.* Egypt	*19.* Ethiopia	*20.* Ethiopia
21. Egypt	*22.* Egypt	*23.* Zaïre (Congo)	*24.* Hausa	*25.* Egypt
26. Tunisia	*27.* Mali	*28.* Zaïre (Congo)	*29.* Northwest Africa	*30.* Egypt
31. Zaïre (Congo)	*32.* Ethiopia	*33.* Zaïre (Congo)	*34.* Nigeria	*35.* Ghana

20. African ornamental motifs

1. Benin, Nigeria

2. Kano, Nigeria

3. Transvaal, South Africa

4. Mali, West Africa

5. Zaïre (Congo)

6. Kenya, East Africa

7. Zaïre

8. Rwanda, East Africa

21. African ornamental motifs

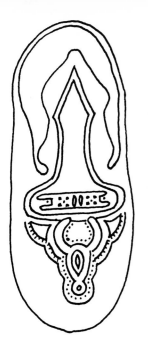

1. Designs in leather
   left: shoes
   right: panel motifs

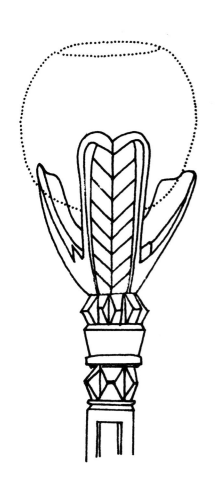
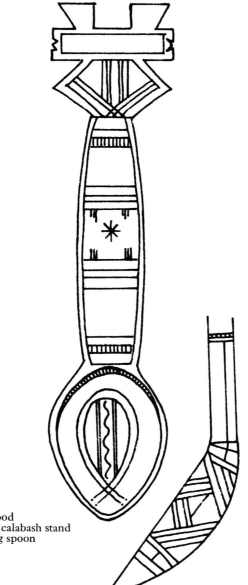
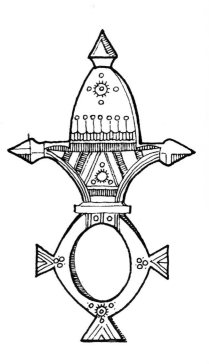

2. Designs in wood
   left: Saharan calabash stand
   right: Tuareg spoon

3. Metal design—Agades cross

22. Motifs of North Africa

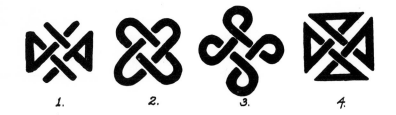

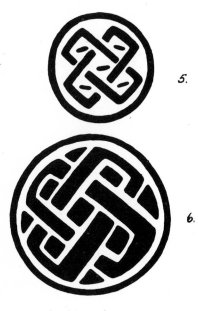

Bushongo traditional designs from the Kasai Province, Zaïre

1. Mananye
2. Mbolo
3. Xylophone
4. Matarma's foot
5. Back of python's head
6. Variation of 5
7. The knee
8. Variation of 7

Symbolic designs of Rwanda

1. Quiver
2. Shield
3. Millet
4. Knife
5. Arrow
6. Kind person
7. Spear shaft
8. Swallow's wing
9. Large tail
10. Large tail
11. Arrows
12. Granary
13. Arm ring
14. Bracelet
15. Spiral
16. Segment
17. Crescent

23. Motifs of central Africa

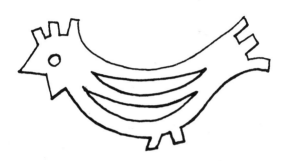

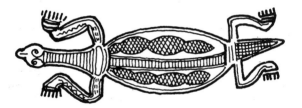

24. *Animal motifs used in African decoration*

2. DRESS

African styles of dress, like many tribal customs and ceremonies, have persisted through the ages, even into the twentieth century. Although the inhabitants of the larger African cities wear western dress today—the men are smooth-shaven, the women groomed in European style—in the smaller communities and villages, Africans continue to adorn themselves as their forebears did centuries ago.

It is difficult to visualize the appearance of ancient African styles of clothing, since old drawings and engravings are very scarce. Some, however, can be found in the journals of such early explorers as Heinrich Barth, T. E. Bowditch, and David Livingstone, and there are several works by anonymous artists, such as those illustrated.

THE TUAREG (Algeria)

Perhaps the most interesting of the desert peoples are the Tuareg (or Toureg). They are divided into five main groups, which are spread across the wide expanse of the northern part of the continent; they are known as the Kel Hoggar, the Kel Ajjer, the Kel Air, the Ifoghas, and the Kel Tadmekket (the Niger Tuareg).

The Tuareg warrior wears loose cotton trousers and a sleeveless shirt underneath an indigo-colored *gandurah*, the long robe of the desert. Across his chest usually are two silk sashes ending in rows of tassels, and his sandals are richly embroidered in red and green. His veil, called a *tagilmust*, is of white or indigo-colored cotton and covers his entire face except for the eyes. The *tagilmust*, which is sometimes a combination turban and veil, is supremely important to the Tuareg man; no well-bred man would remove his veil before women, old people, or strangers within his own society. Even when eating, he will often pass his spoon under it.

The Tuareg's hair is worn long, and is braided into one or more plaits. His favorite color is indigo, the dye of which comes off the clothing onto his skin; this explains why the Tuaregs are often referred to as the "blue men." For ornament, the upper-class Tuareg wears a stone bracelet, a silver ring, and sometimes an elaborately designed wrought-iron key. The key is worn for its decorative value, as well as for opening saddlebags or boxes. Weapons consist of a long spear, a sword (*takuba*) made of steel, and a dagger worn along the arm above the elbow.

The upper-class Tuareg woman always parts her hair in the middle and wears it in long plaits. Her undergarments are very long and white, almost entirely concealed by a large draped cloth which covers her whole body. Her trinkets are always silver bracelets, rings on her fingers and in her hair, and large triangular breastplates. For special ceremonies, the Tuareg women dye their eyelids and eyebrows with antimony.

25. Opposite: An eighteenth-century French view of African costumes

Negre Anzikos armé en guerre.

Femme de la Suite du Roy de Loango.

Gentilhomme du Royaume d'Aardra

Esclave Favori du Roi de Congo.

26. *Typical male Tuareg dress (Algeria)*

THE HAUSA *(Northern Nigeria)*

Not far from the lands of the nomadic Tuareg live the Hausa of Nigeria, who are perhaps descended from the Tuareg but lead a far different kind of life and wear a different style of dress. The Hausa are particularly well known for their distinctive cape-like garments, or caftans, richly embroidered with designs whose significance has puzzled historians for years. Heinrich Barth, who explored the region in 1850, described Hausa clothing in detail and even mentioned his purchase of a "guinea-hen shirt," but there is no word about the significance of the embroidered symbols.

The art historian David Heathcote has written: "The precise origins of many of the motifs used in Hausa embroidery will probably never be known. Variations of some, such as the *dagi* (knot) [fig. 29], can be found in various parts of Africa which are far removed from one another. Some of the motifs have been favorites for a long time. Some of the shapes also occur in Hausa body decorations, as well as in the ornamentation of calabash, basketware, leatherwork, and the interior and exterior walls of decorated buildings. . . . Significant connections may be found between embroidery motifs and certain charm signs. The use of charms is very common in Hausaland, and 'charm clothes,' into which potent phrases written on paper are sewn, though not common, can still be bought." *

* David Heathcote, "Hausa Embroidered Dress," *African Arts*, vol. V, no. 4 (summer 1972), Los Angeles, p. 15.

27. Male and female Tuareg dress

28. Traditional Hausa dress (Southern Niger and Northern Nigeria)

29. Dagi knot, a traditional West African motif

THE YORUBA (Nigeria-Dahomey)

The *agbada* dress is the most popular everyday wear of the Yoruba men and is the common gown throughout western Nigeria. It is usually made of locally woven cotton cloth, and striped patterns are favored; bright, hot colors are seldom used. The *agbada* is cut in a simple square with full, loose sleeves. The neck and front are embroidered with a rich, intricate pattern of contrasting color (gold is a favorite) and is applied today by an ordinary sewing machine. Wealthy men sometimes employ expert embroiderers to do the work by hand.

The trousers are always very full and end just above the ankle. The Yoruba prefer wearing backless slippers with the *agbada*, the color matching the embroidery on the gown; these slippers are usually made of beaded wool. Caps are worn at many different angles and are often made of the same material as the gown. In very hot weather, the sides of the wide sleeves are folded back over the shoulders in order to expose the open sides and to allow the air to circulate. Another name given to the *agbada* in other West African countries is *shokoto*.

The Yoruba woman's dress is different from that worn in other parts of Africa. The married woman usually wears a very large and elaborate head tie (*gele*), and there are several styles of tying. As a general rule, a woman's status in society can be determined by her style of dress, and many times the head tie alone will indicate to what region or group she belongs.

The Yoruba blouse (*buba*) is of simple design, with very full three-quarter-length sleeves. The wrapper (*iro*), of the traditional color "Yoruba blue," is much shorter than that worn by northern or eastern women, and is wrapped around the body so that it hangs in points and uneven lengths.

The head tie shown in color plate 4 is of hand-woven silk and cotton, the blouse is of sheer imported cotton, and the wrapper has been designed and printed locally by the *planji* method (see page 95); the head tie is made of strips ten yards long, and the wrapper contains sixteen yards. The women of northern Nigeria wear no blouses. Their wrappers are draped high, leaving the neck and upper body bare.

THE ASHANTI (Ghana)

Although many inhabitants of Ghana wear modern western dress, the national costume of the country is the traditional robe, made of woven Kente cloth. It is believed that Kente cloth was introduced into the Ashanti country in the seventeenth century, when an Ashanti chief, Oti Akenter, noticed among the goods of the Arab traders decorative patterns and bright colors of certain unusual silks. Cloth strip weaving had already been established in Ghana, so it was a simple matter for the chief to order the adaptation of traditional tools and equipment to develop the bright, richly designed material now known as Kente. The designs are traditional, each pattern having a different meaning, and some representing particular clans or social ranks. For many years the wearing of Kente was restricted to royalty, and each king or chief wore his own commissioned design. The old pattern names are still used, one cloth usually being made up of several different patterns, but today anyone in Ghana can wear a Kente cloth. In recent years, women have created new patterns and styles for their own use.

1. *Tuareg (Algeria)*

TRIBAL DRESS

2. *Hausa (Niger)*

3. Yoruba women and child

4. *Agbada gown worn by a Yoruba man (Nigeria)*

39

5. *Ashanti man wearing Kente robe (Ghana)*

6. *A Masai bride (Kenya)*

7. *The* boubou *(or* bubu*) is a robe worn by the women of Senegal, Mali, Guinea, and Upper Volta.*

42

8. The Basuto are noted for their colorful handmade
blankets and woven hats (South Africa)

9. The married Ndebele woman's costume is made of black leather and decorated with beads (South Africa)

10. Like the Herero, Lozi women dress in a manner adapted from the clothes of Victorian missionaries (South Africa)

11. *Above left: A typical headdress worn by a Pondo woman*
Above right: A Baca headdress
Left: A Swazi youth in courting attire

30. Government officials of Ghana wearing traditional Kente cloth garments

31. Senegalese women at market

THE MASAI (Kenya-Tanzania)

The Masai people live in southern Kenya and northern Tanzania, surrounded by Bantu territory; they subsist exclusively by animal husbandry and hunting.

The headdress of the Masai warriors or hunters is called an *olowaru*. Made from a lion's mane, it may be worn only by the *moran* (junior warriors) who have caught lions single-handedly. Other warriors may wear ostrich-plumed headpieces. Masai men perforate their ears, stretching the lobes with wooden plugs and copper weights.

They also wear beaded necklaces, bracelets, and beaded earrings looped through the cartilage of the upper ear. Their heavily greased and red-ochred hair is braided in pigtails; their ochre-painted bodies are partially covered by about two yards of ochre-dyed calico or hide, which is usually knotted over one shoulder.

Masai girls and women wear heavy arm and leg decorations of iron, copper, or brass wire bought from the traders. They make these ornaments themselves, using no tools (see fig. 187). Their massive earrings proclaim: "I am a married woman." The Masai wife tries never to let her husband see her without her huge ornaments.

32. *A Masai warrior (Kenya)*

33. *A Masai chief*

47

THE BUSHMEN *(Southwest Africa)*

The Bushman woman wears a frontal apron of supple leather edged with ostrich shell beads. A rear skirt is sometimes worn; this is of leather and reaches to the calves of the legs. A *kaross*, tied on the right shoulder and passed under the left arm, is secured to the side by a leather thong, thus forming a pouch in which to carry a baby or food gathered from the veld. Hung from the woman's neck is the shell of a Kalahari tortoise, blocked at one end with beeswax to make a powder box and decorated with eggshell beads.

In this box is stored aromatic powdered root and a piece of soft leather with which to apply it to the neck and shoulders; the perfume of this powder is strangely exhilarating in the desert heat. The woman also wears beads around her hips and neck, and threaded into her hair in long, flat panels or medallions. Her hair, short and similar in texture to that of the Bantu, is worn in a thick mat with bead ornaments hanging from its fringes. Many armbands of animal skin are worn to boast of a husband skilled in hunting.

The male Bushman traditionally wears only a loincloth, and occasionally a beaded bracelet made of ostrich shell or wood.

34. A Bushman woman

35. A Bushman mother and child (South Africa)

36. *The Herero woman still wears the style of clothes introduced by English and German missionaries in the nineteenth century (Namibia, South Africa)*

THE HERERO (Southwest Africa)

The everyday attire of the Herero woman consists of a high headdress and an "Empire style" frock with a short bodice, long sweeping skirts, and leg-o'-mutton sleeves. This style of dress is said to have originated with the wives of early missionaries. The Herero turban is put on at the age of eighteen to signify readiness for marriage.

THE BASUTO (South Africa)

The Basuto people of the Transvaal region swathe themselves in bright blankets of red and indigo, sky blue and yellow, usually patterned in geometric designs. They show great skill in weaving their conical hats.

THE PEDI (Southeast Africa)

The Pedi women wear smocks of enormous proportions with big sleeves. These colorful smocks are decorated with stripes, and over them are worn aprons of goatskin which carry beaded medallions and fringes. The women also wear many bracelets and anklets, which are usually loose strands of large and small beads. The hair is worn like a pancake of teased-out strands, bound inward at the edges. When fully dressed, the Pedi women wear magnificent head cloths tied in spectacular styles.

49

37. The Basuto are easily recognized by their blankets and handmade straw hats (Basutoland, South Africa)

38. A Basuto man

39. Pedi women (Transvaal)

XHOSA

The Bantu tribes of South Africa originally included three main groups, the Thonga, Shona, and Nguni. The Nguni moved far south, scattering in many directions to form the Zulu, Swazi, Xhosa, Ndebele, and Fingo. Each tribe is as different as individuals in a village, but as people of a common stock, they live with common denominators in their customs, though details may differ. The Xhosa group is very interesting with their colorful ochred faces and golden blankets decorated with blue beads, buttons, and braid. The blankets are colored by beating various shades of ochre into the cloth texture.

When the Zulu became the conquerors of the Natal area of South Africa, the Xhosa settled in the green hills of the Transkei.

PONDO

The Pondo taste for dress is quieter than that of their Zulu neighbors. Their beadwork design is restrained, usually fashioned in blue and white in contrast to the bright, colorful gaiety of Zulu beading. Both the men and the women wear many rings, bangles, and anklets. The women's ceremonial costume is distinctly plain, with colored accents carried out by bright beaded pins which fasten their head ties (see color plate 11). Pondo men favor red ochred blankets beaded in the favorite blue and white.

51

40. *A Xhosa woman with a clay pipe (South Africa)*

41. *Pondo women making bead necklaces (Natal, South Africa)*

52

CEREMONIAL COSTUME

12. *An emir of Northern Nigeria*

54

13. Poro Society costumes of Liberia

14. An Ibo ceremonial costume (Nigeria)

15. This kanaga *mask is one of more than
eighty variations worn by the Dogon (Mali)*

16. *A Nigerian drummer wearing a* dashiki

17. *Fali women of Northern Nigeria and Chad*

57

18. *Ceremonial costumes of Zaire*

58

19. *Stilt dancers of the Dan tribe (Ivory Coast)*

20. *A Guinean ceremonial costume*

21. Watusi dancer and apprentice (Rwanda)

3. CEREMONIAL COSTUME

In spite of the widespread practice of Islam and Christianity today in Africa, a great many Africans still hold fast to their ancient cults and faiths. So one may find a church, mosque, and "juju" grove or shrine in close proximity, with the celebrations or festivals of each going on undisturbed by the others.

Some of the native African festivals are celebrated in the form of plays, usually devoted to some great man of the past: a king, a chief, a warrior, or simply a man held in great esteem. Some plays depict the spirits of the ancestors returning to bless the people, to give them help, or perhaps even to pass judgment on wrongdoers. Other plays are simply traditional ceremonies connected with initiation rites or with the installation of chiefs, the latter involving the presentation of stools, swords, gifts, and other symbols of office. Seedtime and harvest, fishing and hunting, birth, death, and marriage—each has its ceremony to invoke the pleasure of the gods and to insure success in the undertaking.

Dancing and drumming are the most common outward and visible forms of celebration, in which all initiated members of the tribe may participate (women are always excluded, although there are places in Nigeria where elderly women with means may become initiates). Some dances are traditionally associated with specific ceremonies; many others are devised by the participants to complement various costumes and roles. For instance, if a dancer chooses to wear a costume imitating a certain kind of bird, he will invent a dance to reproduce faithfully the movements of the creature he is portraying.

Many of the dances involve wearing special masks together with elaborate costumes. These serve not only to disguise the performer but also to convey the attributes of the personage or thing portrayed. Among Nigerians, particularly the Ibo, masquerades are used to invoke ancestral spirits—gods, visitors from the world of the dead, or certain legendary heroes.

In some areas of West Africa, tribal customs are governed by secret societies. The most dominant of these groups is the all powerful Poro Society of Liberia, which plays a strong role in all aspects of village community life, particularly in religion and politics. The Poro Society attends to ancestral sanctions, settles disputes, establishes market prices, and is responsible for the creation and use of various types of ceremonial masks and costumes. The identities of the Poro leaders are hidden during rituals by elaborate costumes

42. *A Moroccan girl in wedding costume*

43. *Alawia, an Arab woman of the Sudan, wearing a* tobe *dress*

44. *Opposite: A Bedouin costume*

62

which usually represent an ancestral guardian spirit. Many masquerades seem to have little purpose other than to entertain, and in these cases, the supposedly supernatural origin of the figures being portrayed serves primarily to heighten the dramatic impact of the performance rather than to convey any particular religious ambience. In sections of Rhodesia and Zambia, the masquerades are performed as colorful tourist attractions, the general performance timed to the arrival of visitors, and the original meanings of the dancing and music lost.

One of the most important aspects of these ceremonies—at least as far as we are concerned here—is that masquerades have provided a major stimulus for the arts: sculpture, singing, music, dancing, and drama. In fact, the artist's contribution to the ceremonies is often as great as that of the individual performer. Many of the masks now on view in museums throughout the world are objects of great beauty, and are displayed for their aesthetic value, though we must remember that the mask or headdress alone, out of context, can never convey the full impact of the ceremony itself, which is a dynamic performance combining all the arts in constant motion. In many cases, for example, headdresses are worn with the face heading upward, toward the sky, so that it cannot be seen in detail during a performance; also, masquerades are often held at night, which further reduces visibility.

Today masquerading has lost most of the religious impact which brought it into being and sustained it for generations, and many young people in Africa feel that it is a fraud. Nevertheless, at first sight it still appears to have all the essence, vitality, and prestige that characterized it not long ago.

THE DOGON (Mali)

Dogon sculpture is said to be stubbornly individualistic and, for this reason, it constitutes one of the finest landmarks in African art. Dogon ceremonial masks are undoubtedly the most in-

45. *Ceremonial costume of the Poro Society (Liberia)*

teresting of their art forms, and one of the best known types of the eighty or so studied is the *Kanaga* (Hand of God), which is usually worn by newly initiated youths. The mask is made of wood from the bombax tree, painted red, white, and black, and topped with a structure often referred to by westerners as the "Cross of Lorraine." Authorities disagree as to the true meaning of the cross; it has been interpreted as a bird in flight and also as a symbolic representation of heaven and earth. The Kanaga mask is supplemented by a fiber costume dyed a bright red and decorated with cowrie shells.

THE YORUBA (Nigeria-Dahomey)

The Yoruba are highly skilled in the art of drumming, and make a great variety of drums, each with its special purpose and distinctive sound. The "talking drum" is made in several styles, is usually decorated with leather and bells, and, in expert hands, it is capable of imitating the

46. *Wooden ceremonial masks of the Dogon (Mali)*

tone sound of the Yoruba language. The drummer in figure 48 is wearing a *buba* costume, the blouse of which is called the *dashiki*.

THE BAMBARA (Mali)

The Chi Wara (antelope) dance mask is one of the most distinctive of African art forms, and is used by the Bambara in their fertility rites. According to legend, Chi Wara was sent out by the creator to instruct the farmers in planting, and each year at planting time a ceremony is held to honor him.

There are many variations of this extremely decorative carving to be found in the upper Niger region of Mali. The horizontal type is generally found in the southwestern area around the towns of Bamako, Kita, and Kolokani, while the vertical mask is found farther east, in and around Segu, San, and Koutiala.

47. *An Ibo masquerader wearing a maiden spirit mask (Nigeria)*

65

48. *A Yoruba costume symbolizing justice and spiritual power (Nigeria)*

49. *Chi Wara dancers of the Bambara tribe (Mali). No. 1 is a horizontal mask; No. 2 is called a vertical mask.*

50. Below: *A masked dancer of the San tribe* (Mali)

51. *Sudanese sorcerers* (Mali)

THE TUTSI (Rwanda)

All Africa sings and dances, but no group surpasses the tall, aristocratic Tutsi, or Watusi, who live in the tiny country of Rwanda, which is sandwiched between Zaïre, Uganda, and Tanzania in central Africa. The Tutsi are excellent craftsmen, and their basketry is the finest to be found in Africa, but they are best known for their elegant, graceful dancing.

There are three or four Tutsi dance costumes, which are worn according to the dancer's rank. The royal dancers, the story tellers, and the young initiates all wear a costume of the same basic design, but the color varies with the participant's status. Some wear white appliquéd with colorful patterns; some wear red wraparounds, and others wear leopard skins. The monkey-hair headdress is the same for all, except for the horn blowers, who perform bareheaded.

At one time the Tutsi dancers interpreted stories of war and carried spears while dancing; the most popular dances were called *umuheto*, *icumu*, and *ingabo*, meaning bow, lance, and shield. Today these dances have such names as the "Marvelous," the "Female Flirt," and "Thanks," and instead of spears, the dancers carry javelin-like wands.

THE VENDA (South Africa)

Venda belief in ancestor worship is very strong, and the important symbol of this tradition is the ancestor bead. The tribal dress of the Venda is the beaded apron of ancient beads, which represent their ancestors and are inherited by the living to honor and protect. The witchdoctors decide which of the ancestors is disturbed and point out the appropriate bead on its wearer, naming the cure, which usually involves blowing upon the wearer's head while performing a certain ritual with incantations.

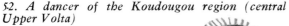

52. *A dancer of the Koudougou region (central Upper Volta)*

53. *An emperor of Upper Volta wearing an embroidered caftan*

54. *Watusi dancers (Rwanda)*

55. *Ceremony of a women's secret society (Dahomey)*

56. *Venda girl drummers (Northern Transvaal, South Africa)*

57. *An acrobat dancer of the Ivory Coast*

58. *Masqueraders of Cameroon*

59. *Beaded ceremonial costumes of Dschang (Eastern Cameroon)*

61. Seat-mat designs of the Mangbetu tribe (Zaïre)

60. Decorated wooden disks worn over the buttocks form a part of the Mangbetu costume; the disk is ornamental but also serves a practical purpose as a mat when the wearer is seated (Northeast Zaïre)

62. A Makishi mask of Rhodesia

63. Shangan witchdoctor (Northern Transvaal, South Africa)

64. A Pondo witchdoctor (South Africa). The white dress and the cap are made of animal skins. The switch, made from the tail of a cow or wild beast, is used during the divination ceremony. The necklace is made of birds' beaks washed up by the sea; objects from the sea have a special magic in Pondo culture.

4. FABRICS

Although African markets are flooded with European textiles, increasing numbers of Africans are again wearing handwoven or printed garments (fig. 66). In Senegal and the Ivory Coast, for instance, men are wearing *warambas* and *boubous* over their tailored European clothes, and even outside Africa, in the United States and Europe, black people have adopted traditional African garments, such as the *dashiki* and *caftan*, and fabrics of African origin or design. Although many of these textiles are manufactured outside Africa, the production within certain countries (Ghana, Nigeria, Tanzania, and Senegal particularly) has increased tremendously over the past few years for both the export trade and native markets.

WOVEN CLOTH

Because of its durability, handwoven material is often preferred to machine-made fabrics. African weavers from all over the continent have developed various techniques for weaving long strips of cloth and sewing them together into large pieces. These methods have grown out of the more elaborate techniques for plaiting mats, and are performed on handlooms of varying design. In west Africa, cloth is woven by women on simple vertical looms (figs. 67 and 68) while in the Sudan, for instance, men do the weaving on horizontal treadle looms; then they sew the garments and embroider them with decorative patterns. Generally, the looms used by men have two shafts which keep the warp and weft apart, and are moved up and down by a simple rope-and-pulley system. The ropes are run over bobbins hung on a frame; these bobbins are often intricately carved, particularly in west Africa (see page 153).

Female weavers work independently and, in a tradition that still survives today, are not allowed to work at all during their menstrual periods. Certain west African towns specialize in weaving. Thiès, Senegal, and Bonwire, Ghana, are two such centers. Most weavers trade their surplus cloth to neighboring villages for other goods.

Kente Cloth (Ghana)

The best known west African fabric is Kente cloth, which has come to be used as the national dress of Ghana. Kente is woven about four inches wide and three yards long; the strips are then sewn together side by side—twenty-four strips for a man's cloth (5 x 8') and fourteen for a woman's. The Kente weavers are often organized in guilds, and the craft is restricted to those whose ancestors were weavers.

The Kente pattern illustrated here is one of many thousands of variations; the directions specified here were figured out by R. S. Rattray, who has made a careful study of Kente weaving, but the native weavers do not write down these elaborate patterns; they keep them entirely in their heads. Although Kente was originally woven for clothing, today it is being used for wall hangings, place mats, bellpulls, and for other decorative purposes.

65. *A Tanzanian textile designer at work*

66. *A Kinshasa woman dressed in Manchester cloth shops for malachite beads. (Zaïre)*

67. *A weaver of Upper Volta*

68. *An Algerian weaver*

77

69. A weaver in Théis, Senegal

70. Opposite: A Tunisian weaver making a blanket traditionally given to brides; according to legend, the marriage will last as long as the blanket

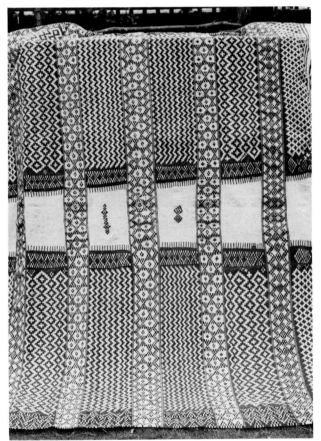

71. *Left: A Berber tapestry showing the hunter's cosmology: the chevron symbols of the Lord, the chamois, and the blessing hands of Fatima, sister of Mohammed*

72. *Right: An example of Berber weaving from Morocco containing motifs found also in Near Eastern art: the star of David, a cross emblem, holy candelabra, and a non-symbolic design*

73. *Left: Hamitic saddlebag used in the Sahara incorporating ancient design motifs*

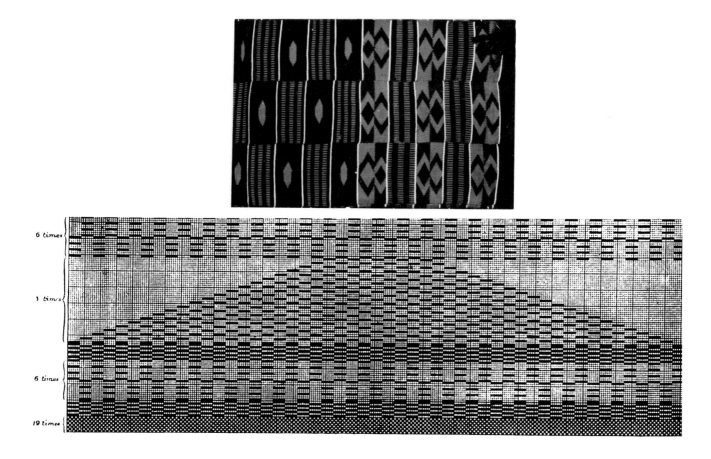

6 times — **3 times** — **6 times** — **19 times**

Warp Pattern

```
 32 Maroon
  4 Black
  4 White
 40 Green
  4 White
  4 Black
 40 Yellow
  4 Black
  4 White
 36 Maroon
  4 Black
  4 White
 40 Opal
  4 White
  4 Black
 40 Yellow
  4 Black
  4 White
 30 Maroon
 ———
306

 24 Black
 98 Maroon
 80 Yellow
 40 Green
 40 Opal
 24 White
 ———
306
```

Weft Pattern

```
      152 Maroon
        8 White Fig.
            ⎧ 9 { 1 Yellow Fig. / 2 Maroon } ×3
            ⎪   1 Yellow Fig.
            ⎪ 9 { 1 Green Fig. / 2 Maroon } ×3
      120 ⎨   1 Green Fig.                         ×3
            ⎪ 9 { 1 Yellow Fig. / 2 Maroon } ×3
            ⎪   1 Yellow Fig.
            ⎩ 9 { 1 Black Fig. / 2 Maroon } ×3
                1 Black Fig.
        8 White Fig.
       42 { 1 Yellow Fig. / 1 Maroon } ×21
          1 Yellow Fig.
       42 { 1 Black Fig. / 1 Maroon } ×21
          1 Black Fig.
       42 { 1 Yellow Fig. / 1 Maroon } ×21
```

```
            ⎧ 1 Yellow Fig.
            ⎪ 9 { 1 Black Fig. / 2 Maroon } ×3
            ⎪   1 Black Fig.
            ⎪ 9 { 1 Yellow Fig. / 2 Maroon } ×3
      120 ⎨   1 Yellow Fig.                        ×3
            ⎪ 9 { 1 Green Fig. / 2 Maroon } ×3
            ⎪   1 Green Fig.
            ⎪ 9 { 1 Yellow Fig. / 2 Maroon } ×3
            ⎩   1 Yellow Fig.
      ———
      537

       46 Black  Fig.
       92 Yellow  ,,
       24 Green   ,,
       16 White   ,,
      359 Maroon  ,,
      ———
      537
```

74. This elaborate Kente weaving plan was written down by R.S. Rattray in his book Religion and Art in Ashanti; *it should be noted that the African weavers do not use written plans but have memorized intricate figures for many different patterns (Ghana).*

75. *An example of Ghana cloth*

76. *The late designer Kofi Antu-baum wearing "his" cloth (Ghana)*

82

77. *Handwoven cloth from Thiès, Senegal*

78. *An example of Akweti-type weaving from Eastern Nigeria*

79. *Opposite: Examples of Hausa weaving (Nigeria)*

80. *A weaver of Dahomey*

81. Weavers of Angola making mats of raffia cloth

Raffia Cloth (Central Africa)

The raffia palm grows wild throughout most of central Africa, and the settled farming peoples make and use woven raffia cloth. The weaving of this cloth was already established when the European explorers reached the mouth of the Congo River in the fifteenth century.

Men strip the bast from young palm leaves and beat it to separate the fibers into fine threads. They string the warp threads on simple looms and attach one or more hand-operated heddles. Loom construction differs from tribe to tribe; some looms are vertical, some slanting. Lower supports are either tied to stakes or left free and stretched by foot pressure.

86

Embroidered Pile Cloth (Zaïre)

Women of the Kasai area of Zaïre embroider traditional designs on the raffia cloth which men have woven from raffia palm fibers. This cloth, with embroidered pile, is sometimes called "Kasai velvet" because of its luxurious texture; it is worn as an ornament for certain ceremonial occasions and at one time was used as a medium of exchange.

The embroidery is done with a needle and softened raffia fibers which have been dyed brown, yellow, red, mauve, and shades of pink. The embroidered loops are left long and then cut on one side of the cloth. Tightly sewn, uncut stem-stitched embroidery, which gives a corded appearance, is also done. Ball fringe is made by attaching little balls of raffia fiber at regular intervals along the edge of a strip of cloth.

The Hausa, Fulani, and Nupe tribes of northern Nigeria are also very skilled at embroidery and produce elaborate pieces of work with characteristic designs.

82. Pile cloth woven by the Bambala tribe of Zaïre, showing the traditional "Mamanye" motif

83. Another example of Bambala pile cloth, showing the Mayulu motif

84. Pieces of "Kasai velvet" raffia pile cloth incorporating tradition-al designs. The motifs at the right from top to bottom are called: "Mi-kope's Drums," "Chameleon's scales," "Feathers," "Knots," "Birds," and "The Sorcerer" (Zaïre).

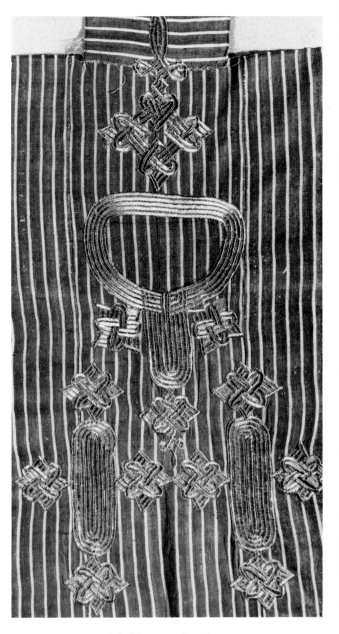

85. Embroidered motifs on a nineteenth-century Hausa garment (Niger)

86. Hausa embroidery

89

87. *Two Hausa embroidery designs*

88. *An example of Nupe embroidery (Nigeria)*

90

89. Embroidered Nupe cloth incorporating traditional symbolic ritual designs

PRINTED CLOTH

In east Africa, particularly in Kenya and Tanzania, printed cloth designs are adaptations of traditional patterns, and they are appropriately named. For example, the Watusi pattern is inspired by the carved wooden quivers used by the Watusi tribe. Other patterns are derived from African animals and plants. The twiga, which means giraffe in Swahili, may depict these beautiful African animals in an all-over pattern.

Several kinds of fabrics are used for this printing, but woven cotton seems to be the most popular. The three most popular designed cloths, especially seen in the urban areas of East Africa, are Khanga, Kitenge, and Fahari.

Khanga

Khanga means guinea fowl in Kiswahili. Khanga cloths are large rectangles of fabric with a central motif, usually carrying a proverb in Kiswahili, and a wide border design on all four sides. This East African dress cloth originated in Zanzibar during the early part of the century when the craftsmen used wooden blocks carved in relief to print by hand with natural dyes. Many of these Khangas had Arabic calligraphy on them which later developed into Kiswahili proverbs and sayings incorporated in the design. The early technique of printing Khangas was probably borrowed from the Orient by the Oman Arabs who came to Zanzibar. Most Khangas are printed in geometric symbols and are 66 x 44" overall.

90. Printed Khanga cloth (Tanzania)

TWALIPENDA AZIMIO LA ARUSHA

Kitenge

Kitenge (singular) and Vitenge (plural) are Kikongo words for the popular machine-printed cloth of Tanzania and East Africa. It is a cotton fabric printed by the engraved roller process and sold by such trade names as Mammy Cloth, Dumas, Finingekele, Java, and African Prints. The imported Java designs, while not in the African mood, are the most popular, and the quality of the printing and fabric appeals to Africans across the continent. Because of the popularity of the Java designs, most modern textile mills in Africa are attempting to duplicate them. Designs from China, India, Holland, Britain, and Japan are also used.

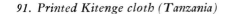

91. Printed Kitenge cloth (Tanzania)

92. A young African designer wearing a Kitenge cloth (Tanzania)

93. A Senegalese woman wearing a dress of Java cloth

Fahari

Fahari is a Kiswahili word meaning "something to be proud of." Fahari prints, directed to the East African market, represent an approach to the "new design theme" in Tanzania. However, the use of these designs is not restricted to fabrics of Tanzanian origin. They are printed by silk-screen and engraved rollers on cotton fabric, and are manufactured and worn in many parts of Africa.

Adinkira

Adinkira (also Adinkera, Adinkra) is a hand-stamped cloth which gets its name from the dye used in stamping the designs. Adinkira

Aduru, or "Adinkira Medicine," is made from the bark of the Badie tree. The word *adinkira* means good-bye or farewell, and hence the cloth is often worn at functions for departing guests and at funeral ceremonies.

The foundation for this type of cloth is white cotton fabric sometimes dyed russet, which is the color for mourning among the Ashanti. The dye is made by boiling the Badie bark in a large kettle into which lumps of iron slag have been placed. The liquid strained off the Adinkira Aduru is the color of coal tar. When the mixture has cooled, the cloth is spread and pegged on the ground or a flat surface for stamping.

The stamp is made from a piece of calabash, with small sticks glued to the back forming a handle to be held between the fingers and thumb. The stamps are cut in various designs and bear Ashanti names of historical or magical significance.

95. Stamping Adinkira cloth (Ghana)

96. *An Adinkira stamp, made of calabash, and traditional Adinkira symbols*

Stencil-Printed Cloth (Planji Method)

Stencil-printed cloth is widely used by the Yoruba peoples of Nigeria. A cassava paste is painted on white cotton fabric through a stencil, and, when dry, the cloth is dyed, usually with indigo. When the dye has dried, the paste is removed to leave a white design on the blue background.

European "African Cloth"

Much of Africa's imported cloth is printed by a wax batik method, and is manufactured in Amsterdam, Holland, and in Manchester, England.

The wax-printing production consists of a series of complicated processes. After having been bleached, the cloth has a pattern printed on it in hot wax which sets hard almost on contact. After the wax-printed cloth has been dyed in indigo, it is stretched across tables and slowly printed again—this time by hand. After the wax has been removed, a range of bright colors is printed on the cloth with wooden blocks, similarly to a rubber-stamp application. Once again the cloth is washed to remove any remaining beads of wax which may have resisted the blocking, and this leaves a pleasant irregularly speckled effect. The cloth is once again blocked with a contrasting color to add highlights before the last washing and finishing process.

1. *Kwatakye atiko*   The shape of the king Kwatakye's haircut

7. *Mpuannum*   Five tufts of hair, a traditional hair style

2. *Akoma ntoaso*   Joined hats, a symbol of agreement or charter

8. *Duafe*   A wooden comb

3. *Epa*   Handcuffs

9. *Aban*   A castle, a design formerly worn only by the king

4. *Nkyimkyim*   Twisted pattern, meaning changing one's self or playing many parts

10. *Nkotimsefuopua*   The shape of the haircut of some of the queen's attendants

5. *Nsirewa*   Cowrie shells meaning "Let's live together"

11. *Gye Nyame*   A symbol of the omnipotence of God meaning "I fear none"

6. *Nsa*   A motif from a cloth of the same name

12. *Kuntinkantan*   A symbol meaning "Do not boast, do not be arrogant"

13. *Biribi wo soro*   A symbol of hope, meaning "There is something in heaven"

20. *Papani amma yenju Kramo*   A symbol meaning "We cannot tell a good Mohammedan from a bad one. The fake and the genuine look alike because of hypocrisy"

14. *Nkonsonkonson*   A link or chain symbolizing human relations, meaning "We are linked together in life and death"

21. *Msusyidie*   A symbol of sanctity and good fortune

15. *Fihankra*   A symbol of safety or security in the home

22. *Se die fofoo pe, ne se gyinantwi abo bedie*   A well-known Ashanti saying: "What the *fofoo* plant wants is that the *gyinantwi* seeds should turn black." A symbol of jealousy

16. *Agyindawuru*   The sap of a tree used in making a certain kind of gong whose sound is said to please the spirits

23. *Sankofa*   A symbol meaning that you can always undo your mistakes

17. *Sepow*   A knife used in executions to prevent a curse on the king

24. *Dwanimen*   The ram's horns, a symbol of strength

18. *Adinkira 'hene*   Symbol of royalty, the most important *adinkira* design

25. *Aya*   The fern, a symbol of defiance

19. *Nyamedua*   An altar to the sky god, symbolizing the presence of God

26. *Obi nka obie*   A symbol of unity, meaning "Bite not one another"

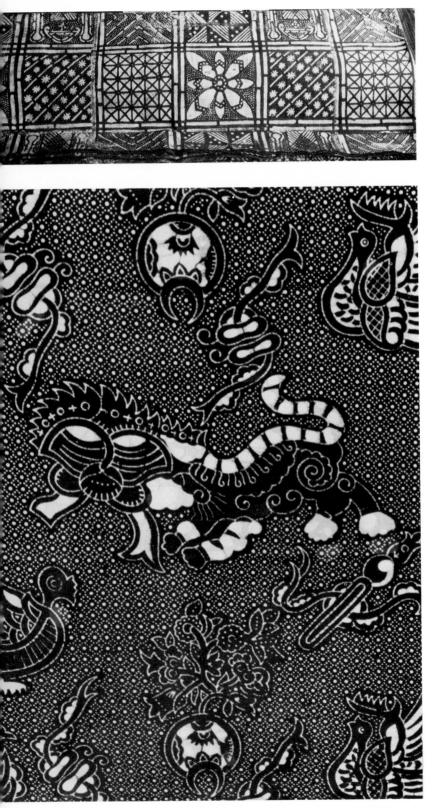

DYED CLOTH

The Resist Methods

Tie-dyeing is a traditional African technique and is used widely among the peoples of Nigeria, Ghana, and Dahomey. This popular dyed cloth is called Adire by the woman traders. *Adire Eleso* means a design achieved by sewing or tying beads, stones, and other small objects to the cloth before dyeing. After the dyed cloth has dried and the articles for stopping out have been removed, an attractive design is revealed.

Another popular dyed cloth is called *Adire Eleko*, where the design is produced by another resist method, usually involving the use of cassava paste to prevent the dye from staining some parts of the fabric. The cassava starch (or sometimes cornstarch) mixture is painted on with a knife, feather, or strip of bamboo. After it has dried, the cloth is dipped in dye. When the dye has dried, the starch is flaked off, revealing the patterns on one side of the cloth.

The Discharge Method

The Bamana (Bambara) women of the central region of Mali produce a fine dyed cotton cloth which they call *Bokolanfini*. In this process the entire material is dyed before the pattern is applied. The initial dye, called *wolo*, is prepared by boiling the bark or leaves of certain trees; after the cloth has remained in this solution for about a day, it is rinsed and dried.

99. *An example of "Manchester cloth" made in England for the African market*

98

100. *Adire cloth from Cameroon*

102. Dyed cotton similar to Bokolanfini (Northern Nigeria)

Using a special mud, which has been left to ripen for about a year, the artist paints the outline of the symbolic design on the cloth with a strip of bamboo. When these designs have dried, the background around them is painted in with a spatula. When this is dry, the patterns are gone over again with a locally made soap obtained by soaking ashes in certain vegetable oils; this solution, which contains a good deal of potash, acts as a mordant. After another covering of the special mud has been applied, the cloth is sun-dried, beaten with a rod, rubbed between the hands, and rinsed in water to remove all mud. The patterns stand out white against a dark background. The Bambara obtain a very fine, clear detail in their cloth by this method, despite the several operations involved.

103. The design on this cotton cloth from the Ivory Coast has been applied with a knife and then dyed

Indigo Dyeing

For centuries the king of all dyes has been the natural indigo that comes from the Indigo-fero plant, which was introduced from India to Africa and the Mediterranean countries about 1600. The young indigo plant is pounded into a paste from which lumps are formed; these lumps are dried in the sun and preserved for the markets. The indigo dye pits are large holes in the earth which hold about three hundred gallons of water, in which the dried indigo is mixed with potash and allowed to ferment for several days. White cotton fabric is repeatedly immersed in the dye and hung up to dry; from exposure to the air, the ugly brown cloth quickly oxidizes and turns a beautiful indigo blue.

This traditional method of dyeing is still widespread in Africa, except in the south, but it is primarily practiced in northern Nigeria. Some countries, such as Chad, Dahomey, and the Ivory Coast, are now using chemical dyes from Europe. Some of the coastal fishermen in Ghana dye their nets a deep indigo blue. Hung up to dry after a fishing haul, these nets are an impressive sight.

APPLIQUÉD FABRIC

At the time when Dahomey was a part of what was known as the Slave Coast, the country was ruled by eleven kings who had huge armies and many craftsmen—wood carvers, smiths, gold and silver casters, weavers, embroiderers and appliqué makers—all working in the service of the king. Even today in the capital city of Abomey, the appliqué makers still sit in the old open courtyard and decorate their white cotton cloth with old motifs, which show scenes of war and the heroic deeds of the ancient kings. Every child has learned the history of his country through these cloths, which often represent legends or sayings of worldly wisdom. One example depicts a fish and a net which signifies, "A fish that escaped the net will never let itself be caught again."

104. *An appliqué maker in Dahomey*

BARK CLOTH

Most of the sub-Saharan peoples at some time in their history wore clothing made of bark cloth, and in some locations it is still worn today. In Uganda, where the best of this fabric has been produced, bark cloth is made from a species of fig tree called *mutuba* in the Ganda language. This particular bark has fibers which crisscross at right angles like the warp and weft of woven cloth. Other trees yield barks with different textures, quality, and color. Most bark cloth, after being beaten and dried, is a light brown; when exposed to the sun for a period of time it becomes a rich terra-cotta color.

At one time, the best bark cloth was decorated with a black dye in bold patterns for the royal families. There exists in Uganda a tree that yields a white bark cloth made especially for royal ceremonies, and this is worn on special festive occasions.

Bark cloth is also the traditional clothing of the Mbuti Pygmies of the Ituri forest. They pound the *nkusa* vine to make their breech cloths and the belts they wear to support knives and other things carried for hunting.

105. Decorated bark cloth from the Mangbetu tribe, Zaïre

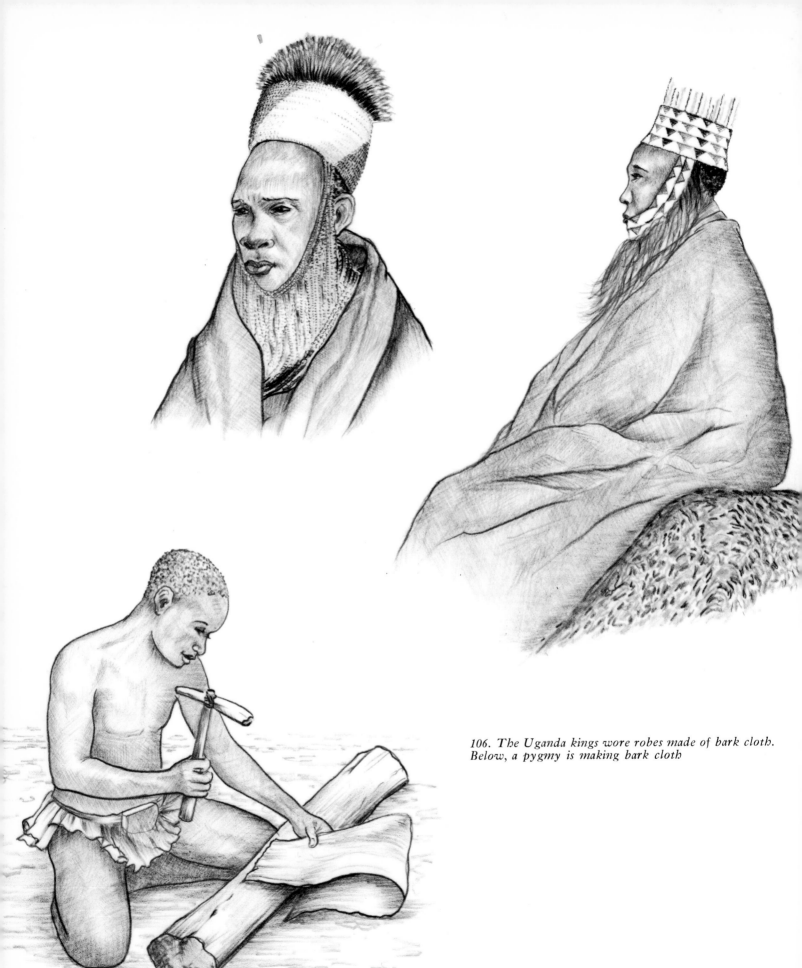

106. The Uganda kings wore robes made of bark cloth.
Below, a pygmy is making bark cloth

LEATHERWORK

Rawhide and dressed leather have long been used by the peoples of Africa for shelter, clothing, harness, shields, sandals, water and food containers. The decoration of these objects has been achieved by several different methods. Thick hide is often carved in low relief in much the same fashion as wood. This kind of hide is appliquéd with strips of dyed leather or bits of cloth to be fashioned into amulets, fans, sandals, and harness. A great variety of things made of leather play important roles in the lives of African nomadic tribes, particularly the tribes of the Sahara, who carry provisions in leather sacks, wear leather sandals and hides, and, perhaps most important, carry their water in *gerbas* (sewn goat skins). Tuaregs cover their saddles with goat skin which is usually dyed red and richly tooled. Their knives are carried in leather sheaths and their tents contain huge, beautiful, decorated leather pillows. Most of the desert people wear amulets against illness, snake bite, evil spirits, and harmful elements. These amulets contain small strips of paper inscribed with verses from the Koran and are sewn into little bags to be worn as necklaces.

Some tribes in Ethiopia design ornate leather shields in many colors and embellish them with brass ornaments. The people of northern Nigeria are particularly skilled in dressing their hides into fine leathers and decorating them with traditional design motifs. The Nigerians tan the skins with mixtures of several minerals and the juices of plants found in the region.

107. A leather worker in Mauritania

108. Detail of a leather palanquin made by the Tuaregs (Algeria)

109. *A Oualata leather design (Mauritania)*

110. *A Hausa cushion design (Niger)*

111. *A Mossi leather worker (Upper Volta)*

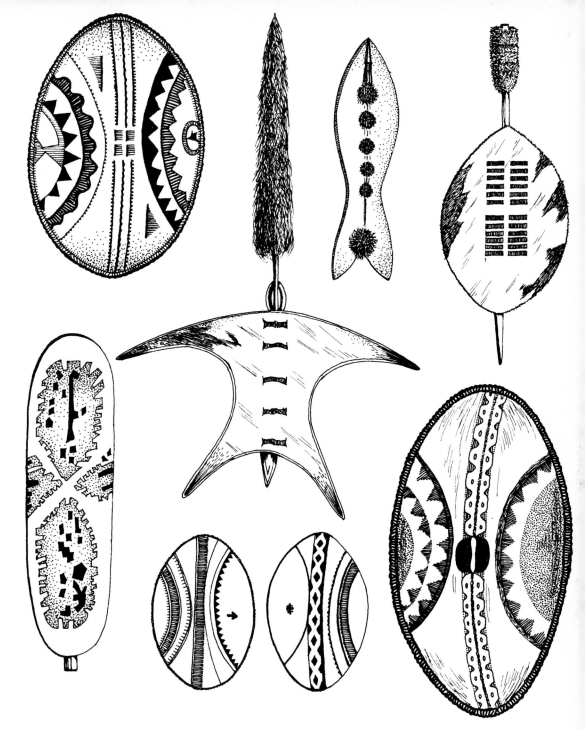

112. Right: Leather shields

Top: (left to right) Nandi tribe of Kenya; Kipsiki tribe of Western Kenya; Lukha tribe of Sudan; and Zulu. Bottom (left to right): Embu tribe of Kenya. Two Masai shields (Kenya) and Sonjo shield (Tanzania)

113. Below left: A Nigerian leather fan from Benin. These fans, which were usually carried by attendants for the chief's comfort, were decorated with incised patterns, rubbed with white chalk, and appliquéd with bits of flannel or light-colored leather

114. Below right: The talking drums (dundun) are decorated with leather; the thongs, which are squeezed to produce various tones, are made of twisted hide (Nigeria)

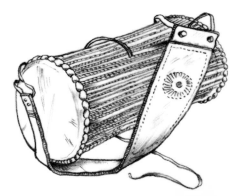

5. HAIR STYLES

The designs of African coiffures from the simplest to the most elaborate are far too numerous and varied to describe in general terms. Techniques include pleating, plaiting, top-knotting, and intricate constructions of clay, grass, string, palm, and cloth. Sometimes these creations are merely held together by hair, though elaborately carved combs are often used along with sticks, rods, and strips of cane to form domes and tiaras.

Some tribal headdresses are so elaborate that headrests are used to keep the hair style intact while the wearer rests or sleeps. In some areas, it is traditional to cover completed hair styles with beautifully draped head ties for traveling outside the village community to the markets or for visiting friends and relatives.

Women's hairdressing requires a great deal of skill. Many hair arrangements are of the same design in west and central African countries, but the Yoruba women of Nigeria use the greatest variety of styles, each region having its own special ways of designing and braiding. Not only do the hair styles vary from region to region, but they also change according to the age and status of the woman. Special occasions call for elaborate hairdos. Priests, priestesses, and members of different religious cults often have specially braided designs to set them apart from the uninitiated. These distinctions are beginning to break down, however, and women are wearing whatever style they find attractive and fashionable.

115. *Nineteenth-century African hair styles as seen by Heinrich Barth in 1849*

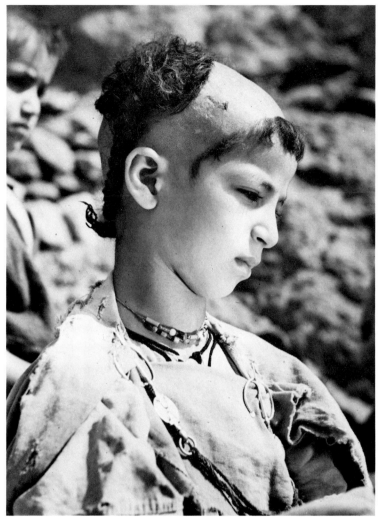

116. *A Moroccan tonsure*

117. *A Saharan boy showing verses from the Koran*

118. *A hairdresser at work*

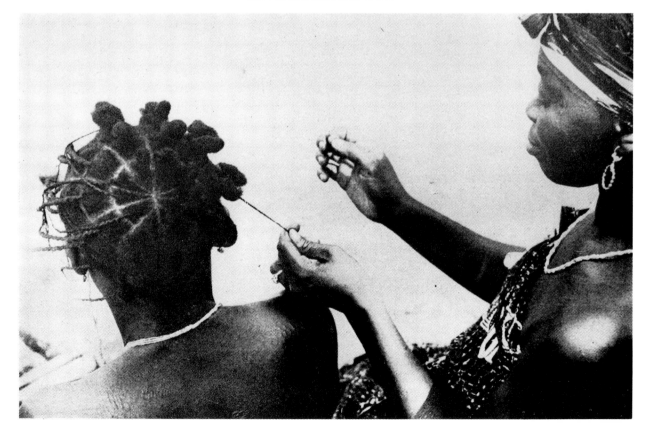

119. *An elaborate Senegalese hair style*

120. *A court dancer's hair style (Dahomey)*

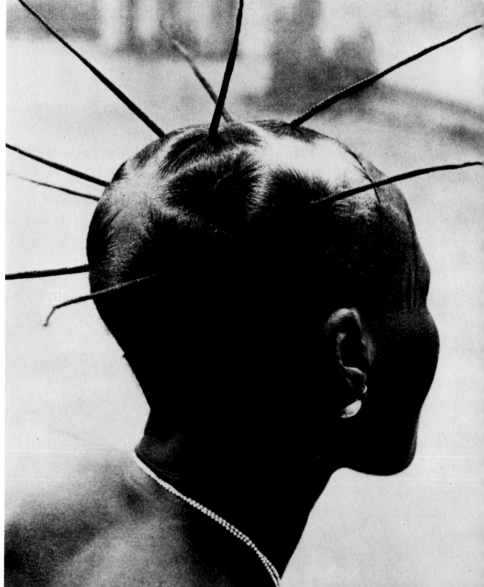

121. Top right: Dahomey; left: Ivory Coast; bottom: Senegal

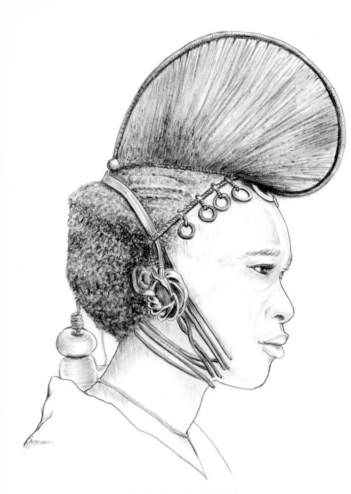

122. *A woman of the Peul tribe (Mali)*

124. *A Kanuri woman of Northeast Nigeria*

123. *A Hausa hair style (Lower Niger)*

125. *A water-carrier of Chad*

126. *A Sara woman of Chad*

127. *A hair style of North Cameroon*

128. Right: *A woman of the Bororo Vodabe tribe (North Cameroon)*

129. *An elaborate hair style, matted with clay and painted, of a Dol-oth warrior (Northwest Kenya)*

112

130. *A woman of the Kaka tribe (Eastern Cameroon)*

131. *A Masai warrior (Kenya)*

113

132. *A woman of the Orambo tribe in North Namibia (Southwest Africa)*

133. *A Mangbetu woman of upper Zaïre*

134. *A woman of the Kize tribe of Natal (South Africa)*

135. *South African hair styles, from top to bottom: left—Tonga and Lonedu; middle—Venda and Pedi; right—Ntwana, Ndebele, and Swazi*

136. *A young Swazi woman*

137. *A young Swazi man who has bleached his hair (South Africa)*

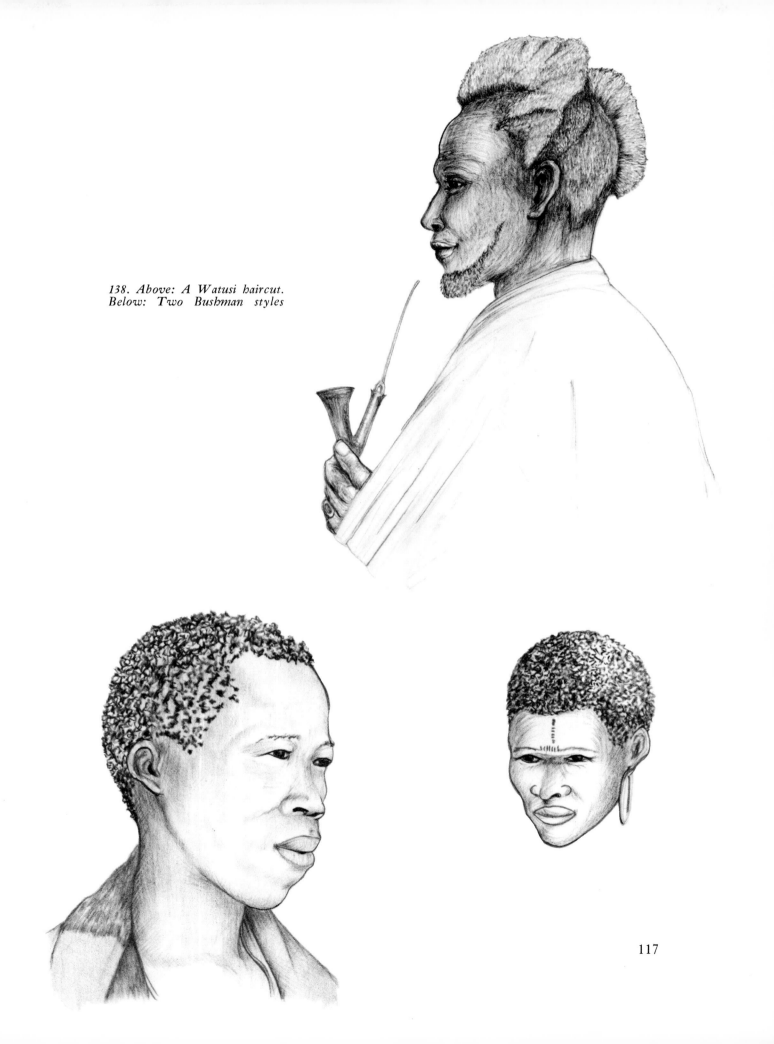

138. Above: A Watusi haircut.
Below: Two Bushman styles

117

139. *A Betsileo woman of the Malagasy Republic*

118

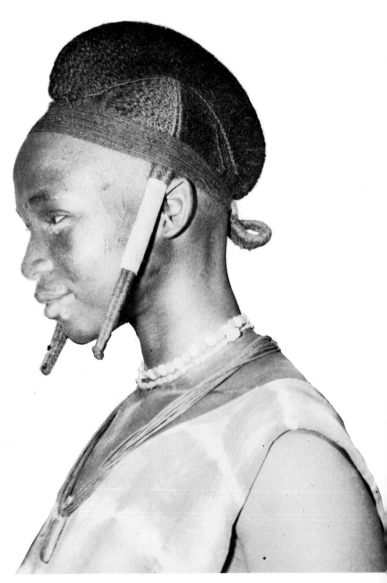

140. *A hair style of Upper Volta*

141. Head ties are often as elaborate as the various hair styles. Top: A Xhosa woman. Center, left to right: Yoruba, Xhosa, and Herero. Bottom, left to right: Herero and Pedi

6. BODY DECORATION

There are as many different purposes for skin decoration, which undoubtedly preceded the use of clothing, as there are different techniques for applying it. Painting and staining the body may have resulted from the simple impulse to beautify, though in some cases decoration has a ritualistic or protective purpose. In many tribes, the body is oiled and covered with color for ceremonial dances, while some groups, the Hottentots for instance, practice body painting to keep off insects, without any evident decorative intention. In addition, body painting may be employed to terrify the enemy or to serve in a charm-like capacity to ward off evil or danger.

The custom of body mutilation, such as scarification, tattooing, or tooth filing, probably originated as a kind of demonstration of a tribesman's ability to endure pain, and it is usually associated with tribal puberty rites. In some cultures, scarification—on the face or some other part of the body (around the navel in the case of women)—is a tribal mark or an indication of social status. Scarification, which is more common than tattooing, takes many forms from tribe to tribe: indentation of the skin is practiced by the Mossi of Upper Volta; scars that stand out in relief are made by the Sara of Chad and the

Hamileke of Cameroon; and raised lumps, like groups of dots, cover the faces of the Ngala of Zaïre. Scar marks may be very light or very elaborate, as in central Zaïre, southern Kenya, and northern Mozambique.

The practice of body scarification is dying out but can still be found among the more remote and less sophisticated people today. Margaret Trowell points out that "it is common to the human race, and to women especially, to attempt to enhance natural beauty by some form of decoration. Among many people this is confined to costume or hair styles, or to painting prominent parts of the face, but the African carries the art considerably further. Living in a tropical climate, he has more exposed parts of his body to decorate and he does this with a thoroughness with which he would decorate a calabash or any other vessel." *

Although to western eyes body decoration seems grotesque, if not actually ugly, Blanche Payne, an authority on the history of costume and fashion, reminds us that these techniques are no more unnatural than the long blood-red fingernails of western women. "The Ubangi woman's lip plug is in the same category as pierced ears in our society; the difference is a matter of degree." **

* Margaret Trowell, *African Design*, New York, 1965.
** Blanche Payne, *History of Costume*, New York, 1965.

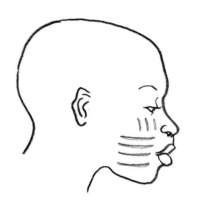
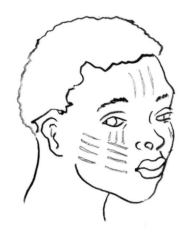
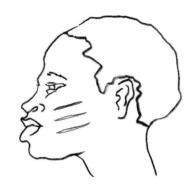
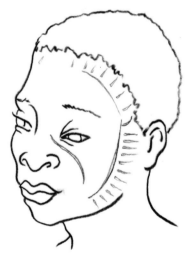
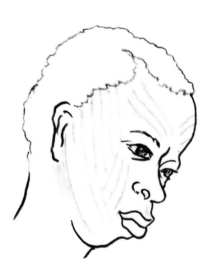

142. Types of facial decoration. The top four examples are of the Yoruba tribe; the examples on the bottom (left to right) are from Upper Volta, the Sudan, and Chad

121

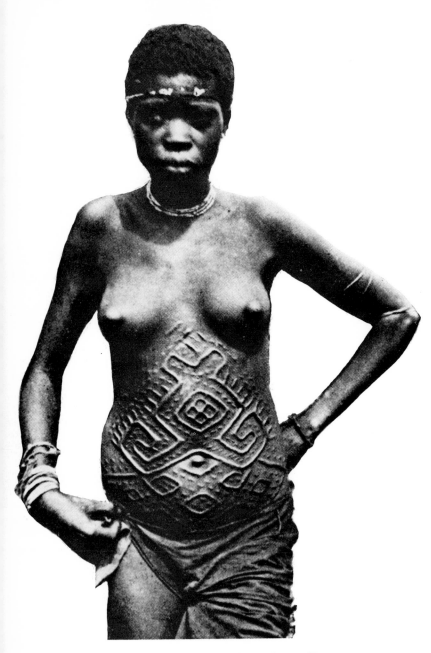

143. *A woman of the Yembe tribe of lower Zaïre*

THE TIV (Nigeria)

Particularly elaborate scarification is practiced by the Tiv people of the Benue Valley of Nigeria, for whom it is one of the most important requisites of beauty. Tiv markings have special characteristics, but informants deny that they are tribal marks like those used among the Yoruba and the Ibo. Instead, they change from generation to generation, though they apparently do not mark lineage. Scarification is begun around puberty and may continue until a person reaches forty or forty-five. Designs, usually geometric or animal patterns, are made on various parts of the body, solely for decorative purposes: men have designs put on their chests and occasionally their arms, while women decorate their backs and legs.

Most of the designs are made with a sharp nail or razor and the wounds are rubbed with charcoal or indigo to raise or color the scars. Nail marks (*mkali*) are mostly superficial, but some techniques (*abaji*, made with a hook, and *umkali* marks) cut very deep and actually change the facial planes, altering natural contours and creating prominent shadows.*

* Dr. Paul Bohannan, "Beauty and Scarification among the Tiv," *Man*, London, September 1956.

144. *A Mossi boy of Upper Volta. In the old Mossi empire, no person bearing these scars could be made a slave*

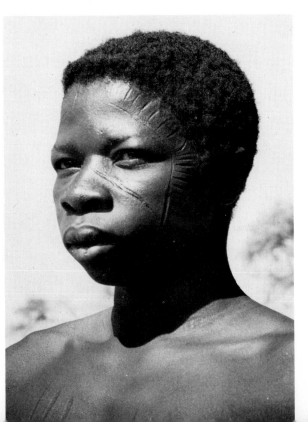

122

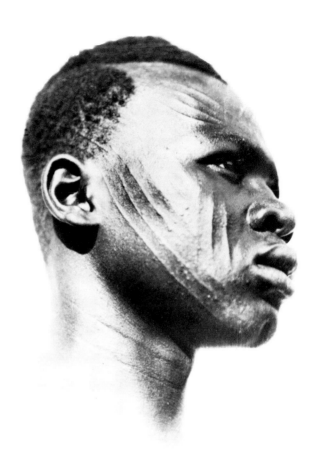

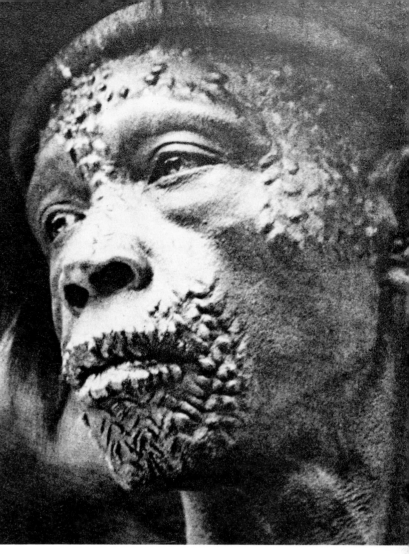

145. *A Sara man of Chad*

146. *A young Cameroon mother*

147. *An example of nail scarification (Zaïre)*

148. *Ubangi women. This custom of facial disfigurement has almost disappeared (Central African Republic)*

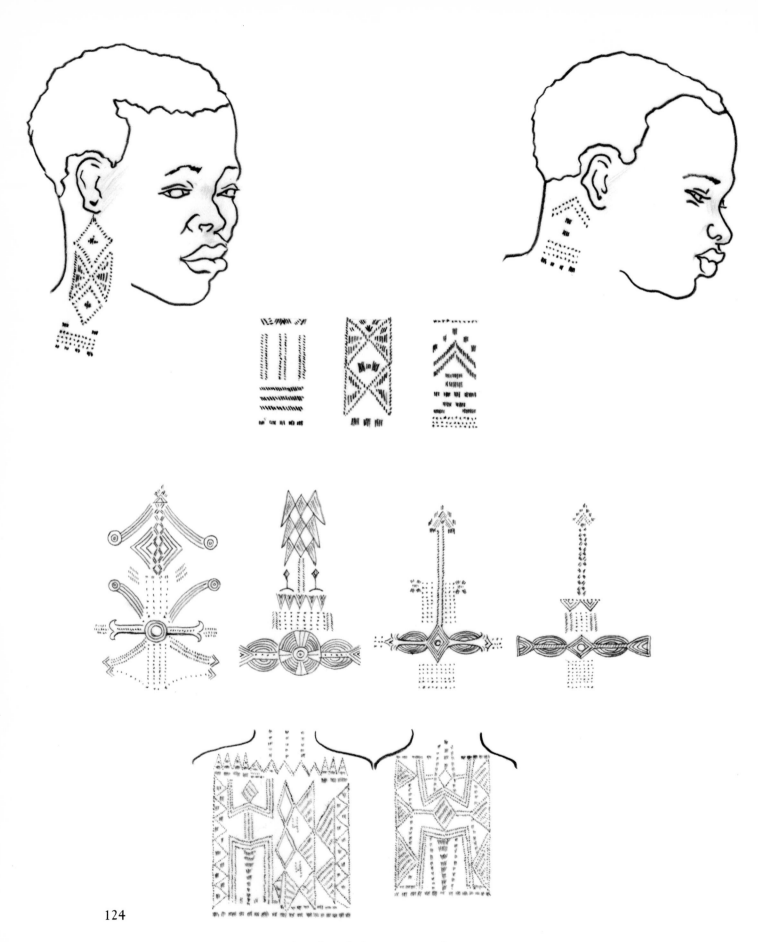

124

149. Tiv scarification designs: top—neck scars; center—belly scars; bottom—back scars (Nigeria).

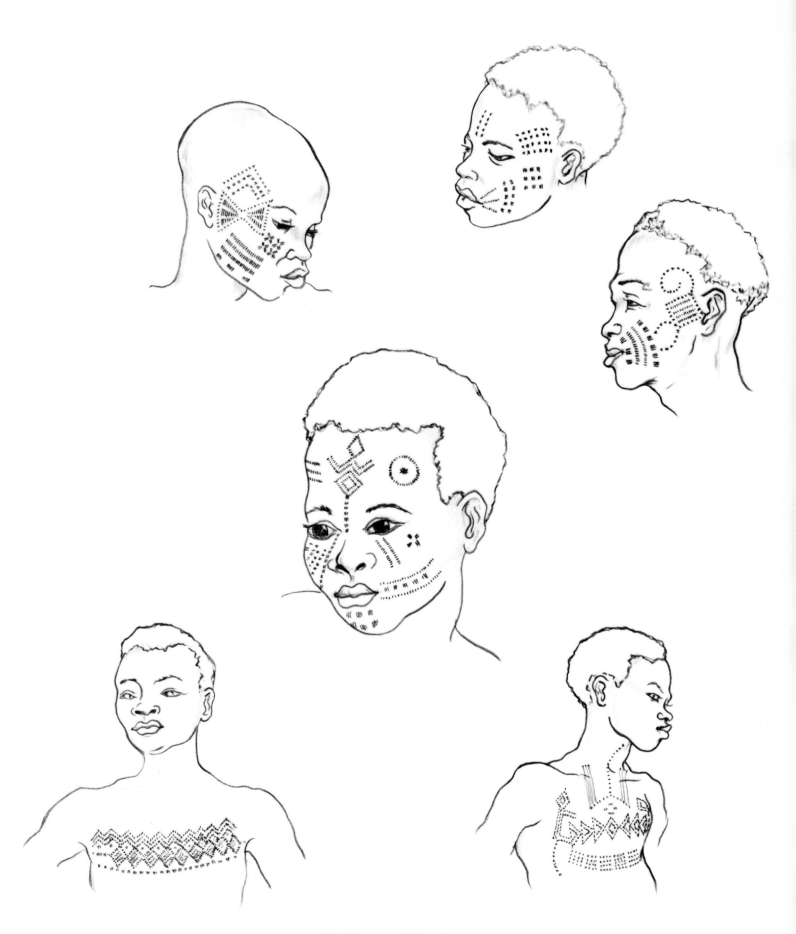

150. *Tiv scars (Nigeria)*

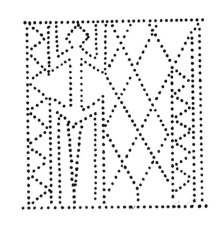

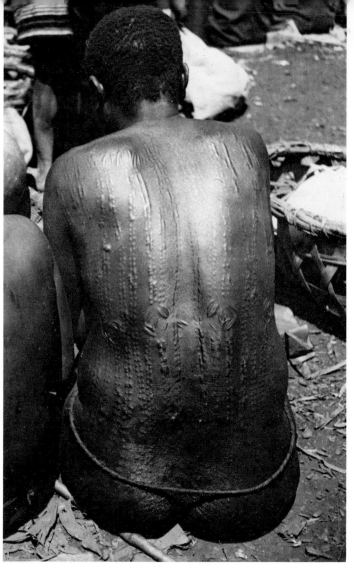

151–152. *Tiv back scars*

153. *Tattóo designs of Zaïre*

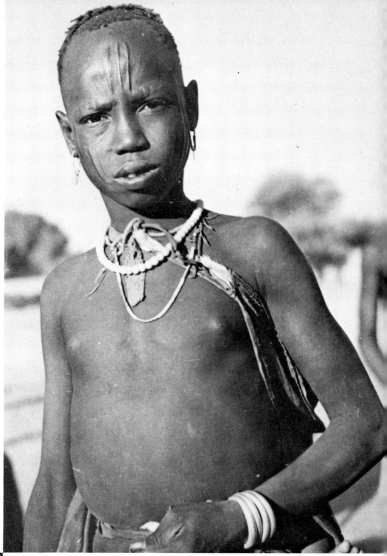

154. *Above left: Cameroon facial decoration*

155. *Above right: A boy of Equatorial Africa*

156. *Below left: Two young women of Northern Dahomey*

157. *Below right: A Peul girl of Dahomey*

7. METALWORK

Africans have been familiar with metals since ancient times, and most historians agree that the Iron Age began on the African continent. Iron was smelted in Africa long before the Arabs and Indians imported it from Europe, and Africans were known to be great artisans in iron as early as 400 B.C., skilled in fashioning lances, ceremonial axes, barbs, and throwing knives. Because there has always been a sense of magic connected with the use of fire and the shaping of metal in fire, the smith has often held a special, if isolated, position in the tribe. Iron and other metals are still handled with great dedication and with much attention to their significance—mystical, historical, or political. Iron is certainly the most commonly used metal throughout Africa, but there are some striking, if unusual, cases in which other metals have contributed to Africa's artistic heritage.

BENIN (Nigeria)

The grandeur of early sub-Saharan Africa has been described in detail by the first Dutch explorers, who marveled at the splendors they found along the west coast. Probably best known is the writing of Dr. Olfett Dapper, who visited the Oba (king) of Benin in 1668:

In Benin the trade is under the control of the king whose agents come down to the port magnificently dressed, wearing necklaces of jasper and coral. . . . The Dutchmen chiefly bought from Benin striped cotton garments which are retailed on the Gold Coast, and blue cloths which are sold on the rivers of Gabon and Angola.

Perhaps most interesting, however, were the pillars he described in the Oba's picture galleries, "from top to bottom covered with cast copper on which are engraved the pictures of their war

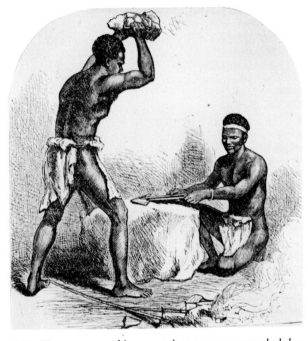

158. Two men making metal spears as recorded by Heinrich Barth in 1857

exploits and battles." These were what are now known as the famous Benin bronzes, which today are scattered throughout the major museums of the world. If they were all brought together, they would present a historical pageant describing the succession of Obas, their warriors, their messengers and musicians, and the Portuguese merchants and soldiers who eventually destroyed the entire Benin civilization.

The plaques and other bronze works created by the Benin craftsmen, including the beautiful Benin heads, were produced by various processes. The plaques were usually incised in high relief with highly decorated backgrounds, representing scenes from everyday life—hunting episodes or

128

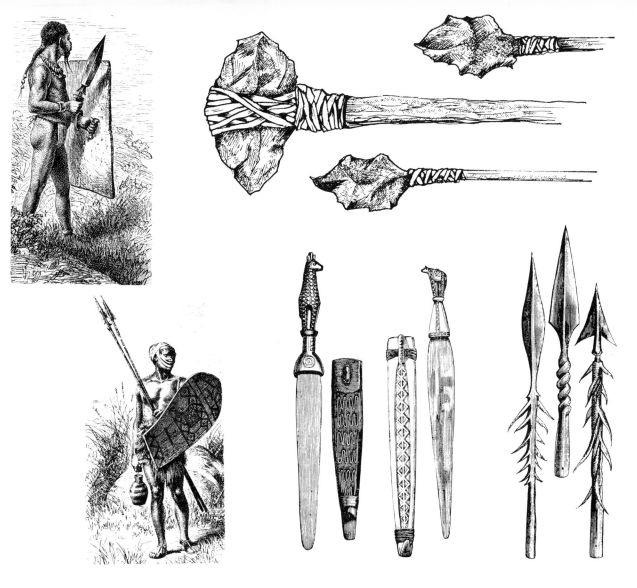

159. *Ancient African weapons made of metal*

160. *A metalworker of Mauritania*

129

161. *Opposite: A village blacksmith in Dahomey*

163. *A Benin bronze now in the British Museum, London*

162. *A Benin bronze showing the Oba (chief) with attendants*

164. *The village of Tada in Nigeria was also famous for its early bronze work*

battles, family activities, or symbolic animal forms important to the Oba, who was responsible for commissioning all the bronze work in the city. The Benin portraits, usually of royal figures, were cast in the *cire perdue* (or lost-wax) process, and rival the finest sculptures of Egypt and Greece in their quality and beauty.

The techniques for casting metals spread through Nigeria and along the west coast of Africa—to the great kingdom of Dahomey, where the kings' treasure included objects cast in gold, silver, and brass, and to Ghana, where the Ashanti used the *cire perdue* process to make the goldweights for which the tribe is famous.

THE ASHANTI (Ghana)

Ashanti goldweights are among the most interesting objects in African art, both for their design and for the skill involved in the casting. Proverbial and symbolic meanings are embodied in both the geometric and figurative designs, which historically had to be approved by the royal treasury for exactness of weight and pattern. Gold was believed to have life-giving powers and spiritual qualities that compelled men to be honest; it was therefore the medium used in rituals connected with the state and kingship. The weights were used not only to weigh out gold dust and nuggets for trading purposes; they were also used as jewelry and as charms by the story tellers, and the symbolism in their design constantly reminded the people of the omnipotence of the king, whose gold was the emblem of the sun, reflecting the light and life of the nation.

The geometric design is probably the oldest form of goldweight decoration, though its original meaning—probably a method of counting—is now lost. Later forms were more representational, and though most goldweights were cast from wax models, inserts, small animals, and fruits were often used to make the casts. Beetles, snails, and nuts with hard shells were encased in clay, and after the gold was cast, the ashes of the organic base could be shaken out. Goldsmiths in Ghana today still practice their craft with simple tools, using the techniques of their ancestors, but their works of art are purely ornamental.

Another traditional form of metalwork in Ghana is the state sword, which is used by the chief on ceremonial occasions. These swords are made of iron, with carved wood handles, which are often gilded. The blade is inevitably decorated with animal figures, or with geometrical or abstract designs.

The *kuduo* of Ghana are made of cast brass, and are used to hold valuables or offerings in personal rituals of purification occasionally performed by their owners. They are made in varying sizes and shapes, some with a solid base, others with three or four legs. They are richly decorated with animal figures, especially birds, but human figures are also represented. The *forowa* is another type of ceremonial pot, made of beaten brass and used for storing butter as well as for certain ceremonies. These vessels are engraved with various designs, but animals or human figures are never used. *Forowas* used by royalty are usually made of beaten gold.

THE OGBONI SOCIETY (Nigeria)

Another historical, ceremonial object made of metal is the *edan* figure, a cult symbol of the Ogboni Society, whose thirty members are the holders of state power. The members, all chiefs and the heirs of their clans, are responsible for the administrative duties in their cities. The *edan* are brass figures set either on a staff or a bell; representing a man and a woman, they are sometimes bound together by a chain. They are cast by the *cire perdue* method and are executed in intricate detail. The faces show scarification and are often flat and broad, the almond-shaped eyes sometimes horizontal and the chin often bearing a beard-like ornament. The body of the *edan* figure has long, thin arms which are important elements in the over-all design of the object. The figures vary in size and purpose, sometimes being used as rattles, staffs, or spoons.

132

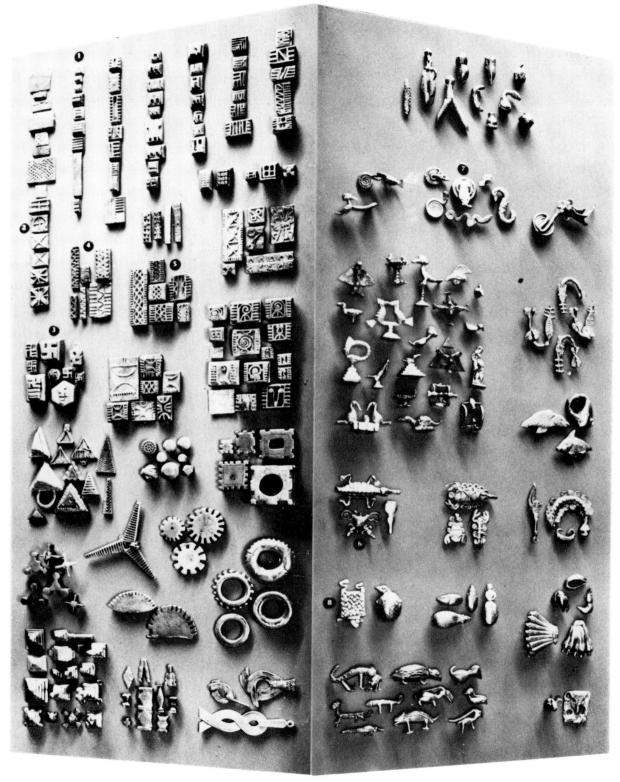

165. *Two sets of Ashanti goldweights, used for weighing gold dust and nuggets*

1. *Nyame*, the sky god, is symbolized by a cross

 9. Crescent moon pointing down symbolizes motherhood

 2. *Mberam*, the female counterpart of Nyame, the creator

10. Symbol of moon and star, mother with child in womb

 3. The double spiral, symbol of creation by the supreme being

11. Double spiral, symbol of Nyame the sky god and Nyankpon the earth god, each creative in his own sphere

4. Female triangle, symbol of Nyame's rule of universe

 12. Arrow, symbol for shooting (shot by Nyame, life— shot by man, death)

 5. Symbol of fire

13. Eight-pointed star combines female cross of Nyame and male cross of Nyankpon

 6. Fire of the sun

 14. Symbol for the day

 7. Symbol of water

15. Kra (spirit) of Nyame. The circle with dot in center; the circle presents turning universe and the dot in center represents the pivot.

 8. Symbol of conception

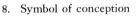 16. Crescent moon pointing up represents fruitfulness.

166. Some symbolic Ashanti goldweight motifs are still used today

1. Hunter

2. Fan

3. Old man

4. Symbol of conception

5. Beetle

6. Bird's foot

7. Double crescent pointing up and down

8. Teeth represent life-giving rays of moon

9. Honsa fan

10. Conception and duplication of mother and child

11. Orosa's head (Orosa: ancient Ashanti chief)

12. Suman (the most popular Ashanti charm, worn for good luck)

13. Orosa's head

14. Swordfish

15. Antelope

167. Examples of Ashanti goldweights

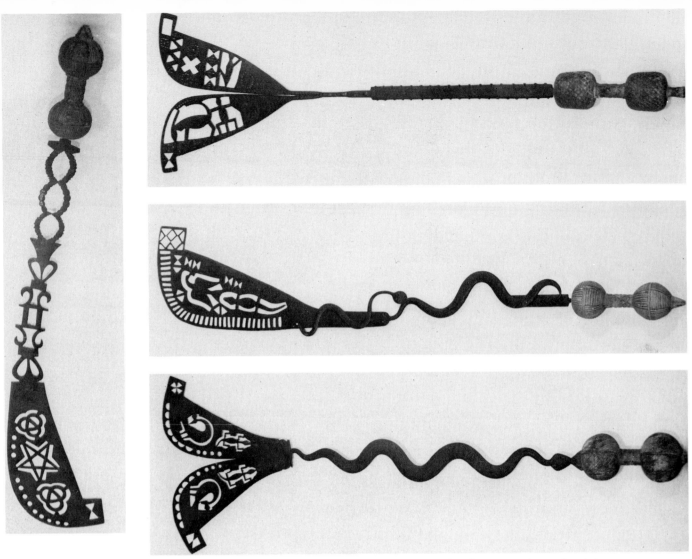

168. *State swords of Ghana. Note the naturalistic animal forms on the three swords at the right.*

169. *A beaten brass* forowa *(Ghana)*

170. *A cast brass* kuduo, *used in purification rituals (Ghana)*

171. *A brass* edan *used to prepare a powerful medicine in the Ogboni Society of the Yoruba (Nigeria)*

172. *A brass title staff is the symbol of the position of the Yoruba village elder who carries it*

THE AMHARA (Ethiopia)

Although the metalwork of West African craftsmen is probably the most striking in all of Africa, not only for its historical significance but also for its quality, metal objects of great interest are made throughout the rest of the continent. The early kings of Ethiopia were crowned with intricately designed gold crowns, studded with precious jewels, and the Amhara today are known for their decorative parade shields, which are made of rhinoceros hide and are embellished with brass designs. The Amhara, one of the peoples formerly known as Abyssinians, are the dominant group of the Ethiopian empire, which is a blending of many races, languages, and cultural patterns. The Amharic people themselves have an elaborate social and religious organization, and most of their craftsmanship is carried out by other groups, who produce articles for them. Ironwork and pottery are done by the Falasha (Jews), weaving and silverwork by the Moslems, and leatherwork by the pagan Faqui.

Ethiopia embraced Christianity about 330 A.D., when the men of the mountains and highlands looked upon the inhabitants of the lowlands as having low mentality and status. To display their pride and to identify themselves as Christians, these highlanders wore neck crosses as badges of identity. Those not wearing the cross were considered enemies of Christianity, and the Ethiopian cross became a patriotic symbol.

The Ethiopian cross, based on the form of the Greek-Roman cross, has five types: the neck cross, worn by men; the pectoral cross, worn by women; the priest's cross, used for benediction; the processional cross carried on a staff; and the church cross displayed on the roofs of all Ethiopian church buildings.

It is interesting to note that, as the seat of government changed through the centuries, so did the material from which the crosses were fashioned. About the sixth century A.D., the crosses of Axum were made of gold or iron, the metals of the region. Lalibela became the capital of the country in the tenth century, and until the twelfth century crosses were made there of copper. When the city of Gondar became the capital, wood and brass were used for most crosses.

The Ethiopian cross is often erroneously referred to as a "Coptic cross." The Copts were from Egypt and, according to history, a few Ethiopians, returning from a pilgrimage to Alexandria and en route to their homeland, remained a while in Egypt, where they taught the art of cross carving and metal processing. Many of the cross designs learned by the Copts were fashioned and exported to Ethiopia, and in time they became known as "Coptic crosses."

173. Crowns of early Ethiopian rulers, now in the St. Mary of Zion church at Axum, Ethiopia

174. *Brass decoration on an Ethiopian shield*

175. *Ethiopian crosses*

176. *Designs used on Ethiopian crosses*

139

THE BIDEYAT (Southern Sahara)

Some of the most attractive items in metalwork made by these people of the Ennedi region of the Sahara are their tea implements. Tea was introduced to the people of the Sahara by Arab traders as recently as the 1930's, and today most of the population are tea addicts. The tea glass is an essential item in Bideyat personal equipment; even if he has no tea, a man always carries his glass, tongs, and a *marteau* in case he should get an invitation. These implements are always delicately engraved in traditional designs.

JEWELRY

Although the types of metalwork we have been discussing originate in West and North Africa, jewelry is made all over the continent, sometimes from beads, shells, and other materials, but most often from metal. Most jewelry is worn for purely decorative purposes, though in some areas, necklaces and belts or girdles have religious functions or are used to signify role or status.

Pendants

The silversmiths of the Kel Agalal Tuareg people, who live in Agades in the Republic of Niger, are famous for a silver pendant known as the Cross of Agades, a very popular item of jewelry. In earlier times these pendants were supposed to possess magical or healing powers, but today women simply regard them as ornamental symbols of wealth. The designs are also used by men in decorating their saddles and saddlebags.

The crosses are produced by the *cire perdue* method. The pendant is made out of a special beeswax imported from Nigeria and covered with a clay paste; the mold is then heated in glowing charcoal, which melts the wax; the wax is poured out into a bowl of water and saved for future use. The process is repeated until there is no wax left in the clay mold. Old silver coins are melted down, and the molten silver is poured into the

178. *A hammer used for breaking lumps of sugar (Mauritania)*

mold; when it is cool, the clay is removed; the silver form is then ready for cleaning, polishing, and engraving. The Tuareg smiths are as adept at engraving as they are in casting, and each finished pendant is an object of real beauty.

Necklaces

The pendant in figure 181, worn by a young woman of Mali, is made of gold by a master goldsmith of West Africa. Because the wax forms are so delicate, often rolled into threads as fine as horse hair, ordinary clay paste, which is used for rings, bracelets, and heavy items, cannot be used. In place of clay, the smith uses finely ground charcoal with well-purified clay, mixed with water to form a thin paste and applied to the wax with a feather. In northern Africa, the metalsmiths of Tunisia are particularly skilled in the making of jewelry.

177. *Opposite: A young priest bearing a processional cross during a ceremony in Addis Ababa (Ethiopia)*

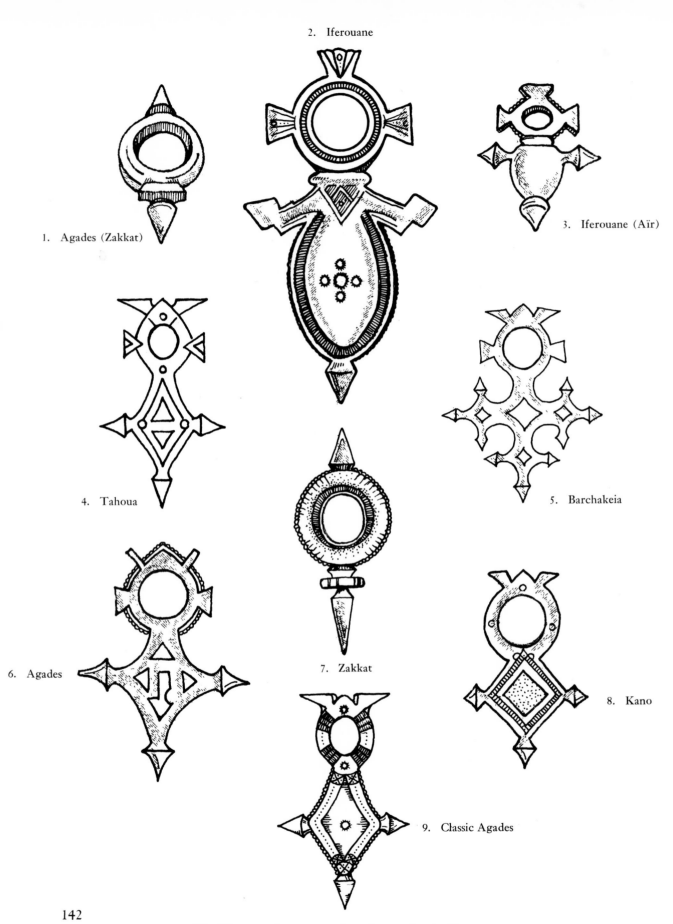

2. Iferouane

1. Agades (Zakkat)

3. Iferouane (Aïr)

4. Tahoua

5. Barchakeia

6. Agades

7. Zakkat

8. Kano

9. Classic Agades

142

*179. These pendants are made and worn by the Tuaregs
in the area around the city of Agades in Niger.*

180. A Moroccan woman wearing traditional jewelry

181. A young woman of Mali wearing a gold pendant

143

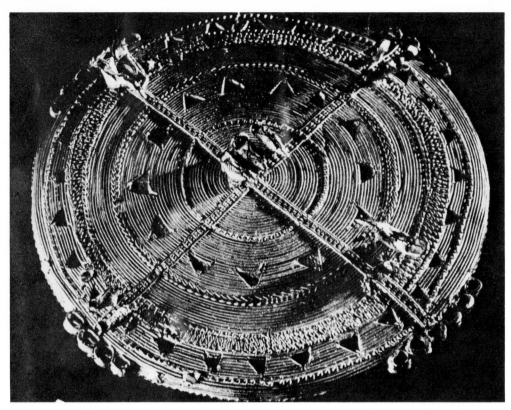

182. A gold Baoule pectoral plate representing the spirit of the king (Ivory Coast)

183. A Tunisian woman

184. A Tunisian woman

Arm and Leg Ornaments

In prehistoric times, bracelets were common, and many cave paintings indicate that leg ornaments, like those used by the Bushman today, were also worn. Although they are mostly decorative, bracelets were once a symbol of royalty and even had utilitarian uses, such as protecting the wrist in archery or providing a defense in battle when embellished with spikes. Leg ornaments vary considerably in design—from a simple strip of beaded leather tied around the ankle to enormous metal coils, such as those worn by the Masai, which often prove to be a serious hindrance in walking. Some tribal groups wear immense ankle plates over eight inches in diameter, though these are now rare. The Hottentots, Fala, Ndebele, and Bassoum peoples of southern Africa wind their legs with vines, leather, and other materials for protection against thorns and brambles as well as for decoration.

186. Brass bracelets made by the Yoruba to be worn during secret meetings of the Oro, an extension of the Ogboni Society (Nigeria)

187. Leg and ankle ornaments worn by the Masai women are often made of copper or brass wire

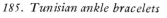

185. Tunisian ankle bracelets

8. CARVING

It is generally accepted that the finest African carving comes from West and Central Africa, from Sierra Leone through Zaïre. To the early African, carvings were not considered works of art in our sense of the term; they were mostly made to be used as implements, often in religious or magical ceremonies. The carved image was not an idol or a god, but a dwelling place for the spirit, and as such, it played an enormous role in the life of the tribe. There were spirits of many kinds—earth, moon, river, lightning, thunder, and so on. There were spirits of tribal founders, ancestors, members of the family, and there was a host of spirits blamed for all sorts of misfortunes, including sickness. It is not difficult to understand how African sculpture served deeply rooted needs for the African, connected as it was to explanations of or causes for certain phenomena occurring all around him.

Although carved objects were used during the entire life cycle of the African, the most important occasions for their use were the puberty and death ceremonies. Puberty is the time when the young male or female becomes initiated into adulthood, into full-fledged membership in the clan. Death provides the great entry into the realm of the spirit; during his life the African is dependent upon the spirits of the deceased, and now he himself will become such a spirit.

Because of the particular importance of the carved object, the emotional investment of the carver is often extremely intense, and this may account for the high regard in which the carver has always been held by members of his community.

FERTILITY DOLLS

Little girls in Africa carry dolls, but these dolls are never considered simply playthings. They are made for children as a part of prepa-

188. A traditional sculpture of the Makonde tribe (Tanzania)

ration for marriage and childbearing. In some areas, fertility dolls are merely pieces of reed or corncob or wood, with no particular human form, though they hold the same amount of special magic as the dolls with faces and limbs.

Probably the best known African dolls are the *Akua'ba* of the Ashanti and the dolls made by the Fanti of Ghana. These are sometimes made by the village carver by request and sometimes by the individual, but they always have the same physiology: the boy doll has a moon-shaped face, a delicate nose, close-set eyes, and arched eyebrows, while the girl doll has a smaller head with incisions indicating a hair style, round eyes, small breasts, and a long, thin neck. The *Akua'ba* dolls are carved to show short arms extended from the shoulders, but no hands.

146

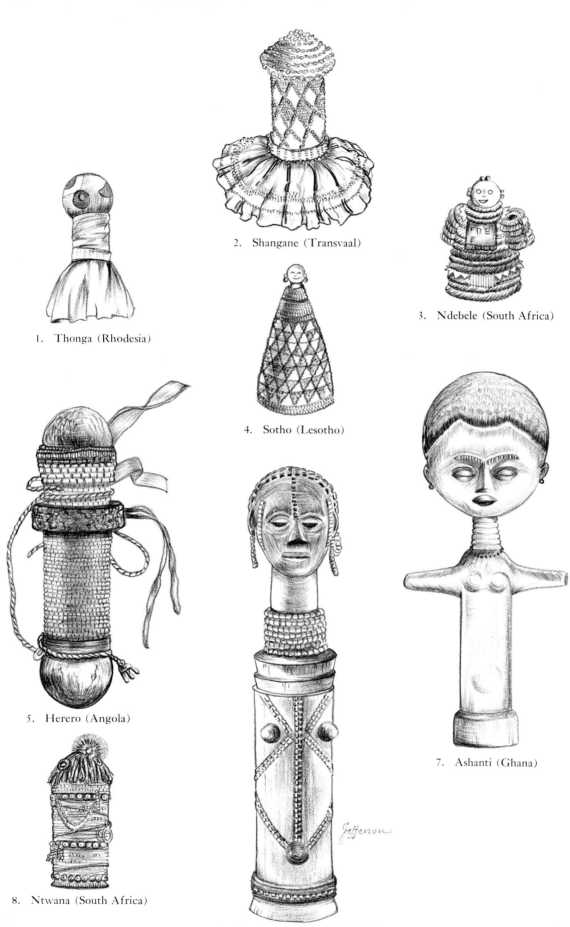

1. Thonga (Rhodesia)

2. Shangane (Transvaal)

3. Ndebele (South Africa)

4. Sotho (Lesotho)

5. Herero (Angola)

6. Mambwe (Tanzania, Zambia)

7. Ashanti (Ghana)

8. Ntwana (South Africa)

189. Fertility dolls

147

190. Right: This tree will make three or four canoes (Ivory Coast).

The Mossi of Upper Volta make dolls of reeds; the Jokwe of Angola make dolls of calabash or corncob wrapped with cord. In South Africa, dolls are completely covered with small colored beads. Most dolls are made of wood, however, particularly in West Africa. The Yoruba women carry *ibeji*, or twin dolls, because twin children are believed to bring good luck and wealth. If a woman bears twins and one of the children dies, the *ibeji* belonging to the dead twin is cared for as carefully as the living. Once a week the figures are cleaned, oiled, rubbed with *tukula* powder, and dressed in clothes and beads. The faces and hair styles of the *ibeji* are typical of Yoruba carving: broad nostrils, large protruding eyes, large lips, tribal marks on the cheeks, and high-set ears. The carving of the hair usually forms a crest running from front to back.

WOOD

The African wood carver invariably hews objects from a single piece of wood. He follows a traditional technique, using a short-handled axe for making drums, stools, and canoes from a single section of a tree trunk. Many wooden objects are used in ceremonial rituals; others are more utilitarian, though often decorated with meaningful designs connected with religious tradition.

191. Wooden chief's chairs (Zaïre)

192. These pieces of furniture were each carved from a single block of wood.

193. *An* agba *drum, used by the Ogboni Society (Nigeria)*

194. *A single-headed drum covered with symbolic figures, some of them* adinkira *designs (Ghana)*

195. *A* tam-tam *drum carved from wood (Cameroon)*

196. *An East African* sansa *carved of wood (Uganda)*

Rhythm Pounders (Ivory Coast)

As part of one of their fertility rites dealing with the purification of the earth, the Lo Society of the Senufo in the Ivory Coast use what is called a *debele*, or rhythm pounder. This pestle is a long pole carved from a sizable tree trunk on which the lower part is left solid and uncarved. The upper part is in the form of a human being, elongated with arms wide enough to be grasped as handles.

When using the *debele*, members of the group pound the earth rhythmically during certain stages of their fertility ritual, which is held at the first tilling of the soil. Dancing accompanies the pounding to complete the rite of raising the earth's forces. At funerals, the *debele* is carried ahead of the corpse and pounded to drive away evil spirits.

Chieftain Stools and Staffs (Ghana)

The most important chiefs in Ghana are the "paramount" chiefs, and though the tribal customs differ among the Ashanti clans, each chief has a stool to symbolize his authority and the soul of his people. There are many other religious symbols used by Ashanti officials—necklaces, bracelets, linguist staffs, umbrellas, finials, and charms—but through the centuries the most sacred of all symbols has remained the Golden Stool. To the Ashanti people it is more than a king's throne; it is the repository of all ancient traditions and the spirits of their ancestors.

Until a few years ago, every stool in use had its own special name which denoted the sex, social status, or clan of the owner. Many of the stool designs were "copyrighted" by the chiefs and could not be duplicated. This is still the case in certain areas, where permission to copy the design must be obtained, but elsewhere the tradition has lost its significance.

Each Ashanti clan has its own animal or bird, and these forms are carved on large staffs to be carried by the heads of the clan at ceremonies, particularly funerals. Other forms—birds, plants, human beings—are also used, and the figures are often painted.

Linguist staffs are carved figures usually covered with gold foil that represent certain sayings or proverbs. The figure of a man climbing a tree with another pushing him expresses the saying that if you do something worthwhile, you will always have supporters. Carved finials on umbrellas and royal shelters are connected with the clan staffs and also have symbolic value.

198. An Ashanti craftsman carving a stool (Ghana)

151

199. View of the late Kwame Nkrumah's stool, designed by the Ghanaian artist Kofi Antubam

200. Clan staffs of Ghana are carved in wood and stained black; the upper part and the platform are encased in gold foil, and the totem is painted in appropriate colors

201. A wooden finial of the chief's umbrella (Ghana)

202. Linguist staffs of Ghana

Spoon Chains (South Africa)

Another form of ceremonial object is made by the Barotse and the Thonga people of South Africa, who carve spoons and chains from a single piece of wood and calabash. During the ceremony, the chains are passed over the shoulders of two people to unite them while they eat from the same bowl.

203. A ritual bowl and spoons carved in wood by a member of the Tonga tribe (Southern Mozambique)

Weaving Pulleys (West Africa)

The weaving-loom pulley revolves on an axle and has the important function of raising and lowering the heddles moved by the weaver's feet. A small ring carved at the head of the support is used to attach the pulley to a crosspiece of the loom or branch of the tree. These pulleys are generally carved from wood for everyday use, but fine examples carved in ivory have been found among the Senufo and Guro of the Ivory Coast, and among the Ashanti of Ghana.

The carvers of pulleys use a double-edged tool to fashion such details as scarification and elaborate headdresses, and the finished carving is as fine as a piece of jewelry. Rough leaves are used to polish the figures, which are then stained in a bath of boiled bark or leaves and rubbed with palm oil to give the wood a warm, dark finish. The hardwoods of the Ivory Coast have a particular richness of texture and color.

In some countries, the pulleys no longer have a ritual or symbolic significance, but the Dogon people of Mali closely associate weaving with speech and the Dogon word for pulley translates as "the hidden word." Baule and Senufo carvers often use the forms and motifs of ritual sculpture, such as the hornbill (a symbol of fertility), the baboon, and the buffalo. The Guro use the antelope and elephant.

204. Weaving pulleys of the Ivory Coast: the one on left is Baoulé, the right is from the Senufo tribe

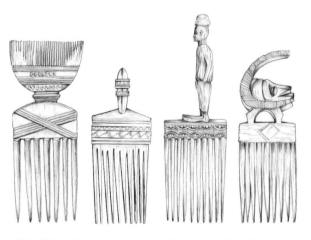

205. Wooden combs from (left to right) Tanzania, Zaïre, Zambia, and Zaïre

206. Bushongo carved cups from the Kasai province in Zaïre

Canoes (Ghana)

Along the 350-mile coast of Ghana, there are many fishing villages, and traditional methods of fishing are still used, though modern techniques are being introduced. Some of the fishing ceremonies are still performed in honor of the god of the sea, and most Ghanaian canoes (there are about nine thousand of them) are decorated with designs expressing the sorrows, ambitions, and experiences of their owners. The canoes are made in the forest region of the country, often many miles from the sea. The completed craft is transported by road to the coast, where the pattern makers then proceed to decorate it.

The Kalabari-speaking people of the eastern Niger delta are also great fishermen, and the water spirit is predominant in their religious life, being called upon to calm creeks and to produce an abundance of fish.

The artisans of the Kalabari are skilled carvers, though their work is seldom visible to the casual visitor. There are no relief doors or carved veranda posts; it is only when one enters the shrines of the spirits that one comes upon a great number of carved figures and cult objects.

Implements such as canoes, paddles, fishing spears, and bidents are decorated with common motifs called *oru nama*, an important water spirit descended from the python. Human figures are also represented, as are water animals, and sometimes the features of both are combined.

207. Canoes used for fishing at a village near Accra, Ghana

208. Ghanaian canoe patterns with trident paddles

209. Designs for canoes (Ghana)

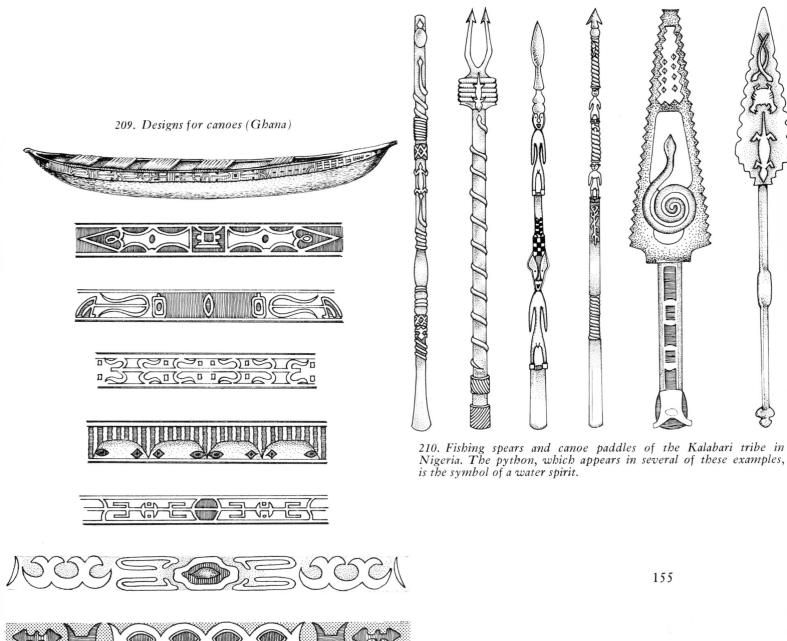

210. Fishing spears and canoe paddles of the Kalabari tribe in Nigeria. The python, which appears in several of these examples, is the symbol of a water spirit.

STONE

Stone is not commonly used in sub-Saharan Africa; except in the Zimbabwe area of Rhodesia and Kilwa (in Tanzania), it is rarely used even in building. The Akwanshi stone figures of the Essie region of Nigeria and the megaliths of Ethiopia are isolated examples of African stone carving. Some small pieces of soapstone carving have been produced in Gabon and Rhodesia.

The Akwanshi Stones (Nigeria)

These stones are an isolated phenomenon in Africa and have baffled experts since their first discovery in 1903. Almost nothing is known of their origin, date of execution, or purpose. They are large representations of the male human figure, made from dolorite or sandstone, varying in shape from circular to rectangular and standing about four feet high, the largest being over six feet. Two hundred ninety-five of them have been found within an area of 350 square miles, inhabited by the Ekoi peoples along the right bank of the Cross River. Many of the Ekoi believe that the spirit of the dead remains in the world of the dead, but some maintain that the spirit of the dead returns to live in these stones.

Fashioned with stone and metal tools, each Akwanshi stone has eyes, nose, mouth, beard, and navel. Ears, breasts, hands, arms, and geometric decorations are frequently incised, and some of the decorations resemble Ekoi tribal marks and local painted designs. Most of the carving ends at the navel, although occasionally a figure eight, representing male genitals, appears. The beard suggests that these are all male figures rather than female. No particular method or style of carving can be attributed to any single village, and the principal differences between individual stones derive from the choice of technique (incising or carving) and from the natural shape of the stone. Several Akwanshi have been found in circles, and it is likely that most of the clusters were originally placed either in the center of a village

211. A soapstone carving from the Zimbabwe area of Rhodesia (Collection of Mr. and Mrs. James H. Robinson)

212. Soapstone carving from Gabon (Collection of Mr. and Mrs. James H. Robinson)

or just outside it. Today, groups are found miles away from any present village, and some single stones have been found in the forest. In recent years, villagers have been known to move the Akwanshi close to the main roads for the benefit of tourists.

213. Akwanshi *stone figure from a village near Ilorin in Nigeria*

214. *Funerary stone figures, or* akwanshi, *from the Ekoi region of Nigeria*

CALABASHES

The calabash is a kind of gourd that grows in many different sizes and shapes. When calabashes are ripe, those that are to be used as containers are gathered and soaked in water until the seeds and pulp are rotten. They are then cut open, the contents are scraped out, and the shells are dried in the sun until hard. The natural color of the outer skin is in the range of warm yellows, which darken with age and use. They may be stained with other colors: rose from millet leaves, blue from indigo, and so on. Sometimes they are darkened by being hung in a smoky hut. Occasionally the yellow skin is scraped off, leaving the gourd white. Designs are applied by various methods or combinations of methods.

A serrated knife can be used to scrape off the background for a pattern, which then appears in relief, or to incise a pattern into the surface. Variations of color can be obtained with a stained calabash, where the stain can be rubbed off as well as scraped. Lines or shapes may also be burned into the surface with a red-hot knife or nail, leaving the background or the design itself in black. Chalk and soot are also rubbed into the pattern for different effects.

Sometimes calabashes are decorated with

215. *A growing calabash*

other kinds of material—patterned beadwork or beads stitched on with brass or steel wire. Soft clay may be pressed into the incisions and beads embedded into the clay.

Most of the patterns used for decorating calabashes are geometric motifs, since the round, regular shape of the gourd lends itself well to abstract or symmetrical designs. Among the Tiv, Ibo, and Ibibio peoples of Nigeria, freely drawn curved lines and leaf designs as well as geometric patterns may be found. The Yoruba, Bini, and Bura peoples seem to prefer interlacing designs with fewer curved patterns.

Calabash decoration is a profession undertaken by artisans skilled in this particular craft. Most of the artisans are men, but the women of northeast Nigeria are known for their superior skills.

The calabash is used for many purposes, depending on the natural shape of the shell. There are large and small food bowls (some with lids), ceremonial bowls, and small trinket boxes or money boxes, the stem serving as a handle. There are also trays, drinking cups, ladles, and flasks for water, palm wine, and milk. The calabash is sometimes used with leather straps to shield a baby's head from the sun or rain. In some parts of Nigeria and Dahomey, decorated segments are found as house decorations. They also serve as excellent resonators for musical instruments such as the xylophone, *Sansa*, or rattle. In some rare instances, they are used as masks.

216. A truckload of calabash en route to market in Togo

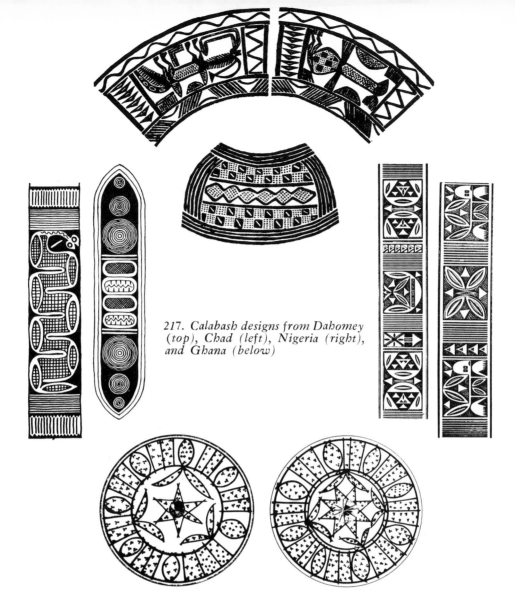

217. Calabash designs from Dahomey (top), Chad (left), Nigeria (right), and Ghana (below)

218. Two calabashes from Northeast Nigeria, the right one from the Tera tribe, the left one from the Pilmidi

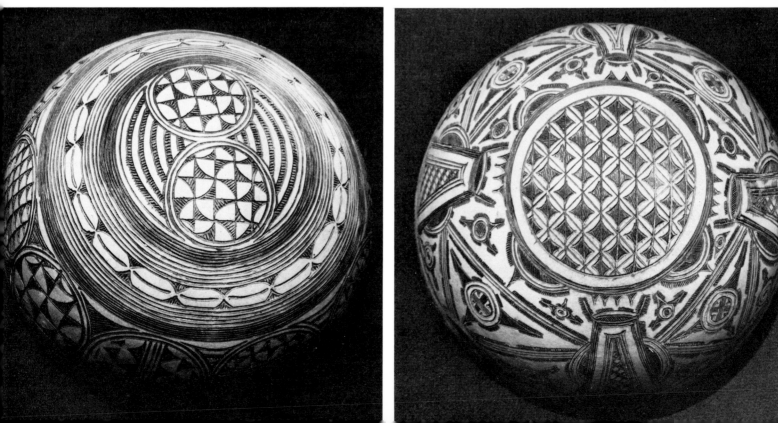

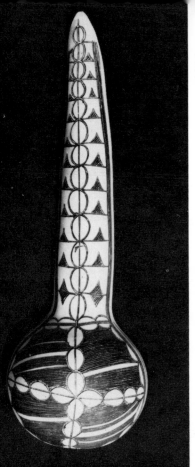

219. *Two more Nigerian calabashes, from the Dera tribe (left) and the Chibuk (right)*

220. *A calabash from Ghana*

221. *A Fulani girl with a calabash bowl covered with a lid made of another calabash (Nigeria)*

222. *A decorated calabash shields this Bura mother's baby from the sun (Nigeria).*

223. *Musical instruments made from calabash;* above, *a South African resonator and* right, *a* kora *from Senegal*

IVORY

Ivory is found almost everywhere in Africa south of the Sahara, although elephants are disappearing from the landscape in certain countries. For centuries these animals have been a source of meat, clothing, and armor for the people, and their tusks are used as ornaments, musical instruments, carved figures, and other implements.

Ivory carving is usually done with the same techniques as wood carving, but unlike wood, ivory may be easily worked against the grain and fine detail can be achieved. Some early pieces were inlaid with copper or brass to emphasize certain features, such as tribal markings or spots on animals.

Sometimes the entire tusk is carved in relief to represent activities in the history of a people or to illustrate stories and legends. Some tusks carved with abstract designs are used by royalty as footrests. Sections of the tusk are frequently carved and engraved for scepters, bracelets, and belts.

224. A Bible story carved in ivory (Zaïre)

225. An ivory carver at work (Zaïre)

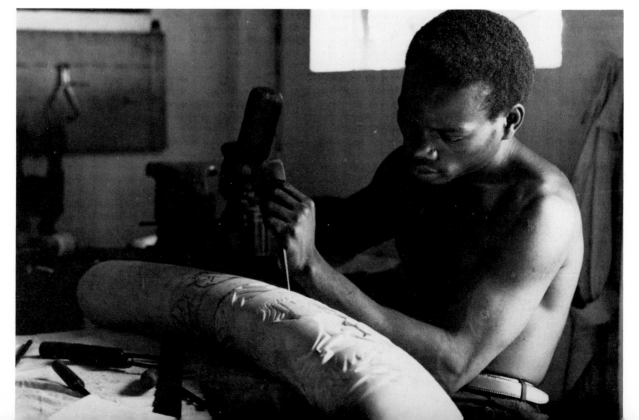

226. *Two ivory scepters (Zaïre)*

227. *An ivory pendant mask from Benin (Nigeria)*

228. *An ivory chess set from Zaïre*

SEEDS

The Kogo, Fang, Maka, and Beti tribes of southeastern Cameroon play a gambling game called *Abbia*, in which carved segments of seed pits are used. The seeds come from the *elan* tree, which bears a deadly poisonous fruit. These shield-like segments are ornamented with many carved designs and symbols representing people, animals, and birds; some are decorated with geometric or abstract designs. These "counters" are usually smooth in texture and about two inches long and one inch wide.

229. Abbia counters made from seeds (Cameroon)

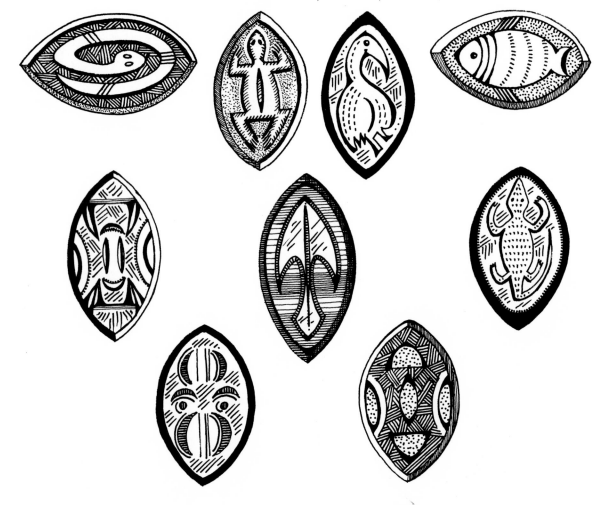

9. BASKETRY AND POTTERY

BASKETRY

Beautiful ornamental baskets are made all over Africa—by the Nubian and Swahili women of East Africa, the Harar women of Ethiopia, the Tutsi of Rwanda, and the weavers of lower Zaïre and parts of southern Africa.

The baskets and trays of East Africa, particularly those of Uganda, are made in brilliant colors produced by the now available synthetic dyes; color in early basket making was confined to reds, browns, and blacks. The Ugandan work is more commonly coiled than woven.

The weavers of West and South Africa produce an unending variety of designs and patterns in making baskets, lids, winnowing trays, shields, hats, and quivers. The men of these regions are expert at plaiting, and produce decorated mats for wall hangings and cushions.

Perhaps the most interesting patterns are those found in Harar baskets, which are first constructed of reeds or bound fibers and then covered with a woven decorative overlay of raffia.

230. *A Peul woman weaving a mat (Mali)*

231. *Basket making in Zaïre*

232. *A Basuto basket maker (South Africa)*

233. *A village basket maker (Ethiopia)*

234. *Ethiopian basket makers in the city of Harar*

235. *Uganda baskets are first coiled with reeds; the color is woven in later*

236. *Bantu basket designs from Southwest Africa*

237. *Two Rwanda baskets*

38. This Ethiopian dinner table, called a nasoob, is woven from raffia; bright colors are used in the weaving pattern.

239. *Woven ceremonial masks used in South Africa: at top, Sotho masks worn by girl initiates; center; a Basuto initiation mask; bottom, two Xhosa masks worn by male initiates*

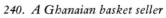
240. *A Ghanaian basket seller*

241. *Bantu baskets at market (South Africa)*

242. *This huge hat is worn by market women in Ghana to shield their vegetable produce from the sun.*

CLAY MODELING

Modeling in clay has long been an important African art; like the making of pottery, it is the work of women. Because most pieces are delicate, however, few complete examples are to be found in museums. Some of the best work that has survived the ravages of time and handling is that of the Nok culture and of the Sao of Mali, among others, but the finest are the beautiful ancient terra-cotta heads of Ife in Nigeria. Interesting bas-relief work is also to be found in several West African countries.

Perhaps the most fascinating clay work is the *Mbari* sculpture of the Ibo in the sacred *Mbari* shrines erected to *Ala*, the earth goddess, which sometimes house as many as fifty figures.

POTTERY

The origins of the potter's art are obscure, and the differences in tribal techniques are probably due as much to the different kinds of clay as to the variations in cultural patterns. All clay contains certain impurities such as iron oxide, which makes some kinds of pottery red when fired, but the women potters are never concerned with chemical composition. They are only concerned with improving the elasticity of the material by removing what impurities they can see, and by mixing greasy or sticky clays with other types to obtain better shapes in their finished products.

There are several basic techniques in making pots, and most potters use a combination of them. The most common method is to hollow out a lump of clay by pressing inward and then fitting the piece over a simple form to finish it. The reverse technique is to fit clay into a hollow form and drive it up to form a high, thin wall. Another common method is that of laying rings or coils of clay one on top of the other.

For decoration, the walls of the pot are first smoothed with leaves and then incised with sticks to make simple linear patterns. Sometimes bands

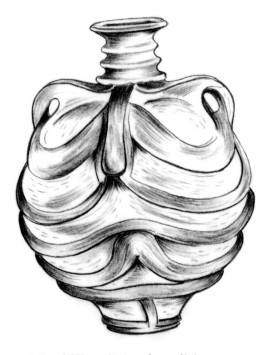

243. A West African bas-relief pottery

of plaited palm or rope are pressed into the moist clay to form a pattern. The Dindi women of Dahomey mix kaolin with ochre and apply broad bands of color to their pots. The Kanuri women of eastern Niger make colors with red clay, powdered yellow stone, and charcoal, using peanut oil as a base.

The potter's wares have innumerable uses—cooking, bathing, burial ("soul urns"), and many others. There is a custom in Chad of filling a small pot with hot coals to be put under one's robe on a cool morning as one squats for the morning meal. There are pottery oil lamps, pots for food storage, pots for dyeing fabric and burning sweet-smelling herbs, and even huge pots for grain storage.

244. *An Algerian pottery maker*

245. *A Dahomeyan woman making pottery*

246. *An early example of African pottery, from Nubia, c. 2000 B.C.*

247. *A terra-cotta head from the Nok culture in Nigeria dating between 500 B.C. and A.D. 200*

248. *Examples of North African pottery*

249. *Two contemporary pieces of North African pottery*

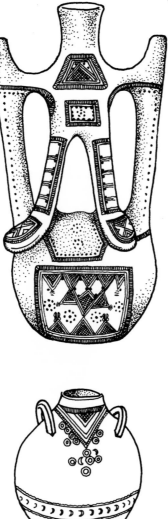

250. *Kabyle pottery designs of North Africa*

251. *Above: Water vessels of Mali*

252. *A pottery seller in Mali*

253. *A Goa woman carrying water*

254. *Pottery used for cooking food (Zaïre)*

10. BEADWORK

The earliest known beads are believed to have been made around 12,000 B.C. These are glass beads found in Egypt which were most likely brought there from Asia. Beads were the early currency of the Chinese junks and Arab traders who traded their goods along the East African coast down to Sofala and Madagascar. Beads recently found in and around Zimbabwe are said to have been used in the third and fourth centuries A.D. These beads differ from any other African types and are called "trade-wind" beads.

From about the fourteenth century on, when European maritime traders began visiting African ports to trade for gold, beads featured prominently in the transactions. Some of these early trade beads are said to have been Venetian, some Dutch, though even before these European glass beads assumed importance in Africa, beads of clay and stone were valued and used. One of the highly prized varieties is the Aggrey bead, an ancient variegated glass bead of unknown origin found in several West African countries.

Aside from their use as currency, beads are used as body adornments and carry patterns of symbolic religious significance. The Ndebele of south Africa are noted for their fine beadwork on necklaces, armbands, aprons, and anklets, and the Bapende of Zaïre use beads in making their *Shene Malula* masks, combining them with painting and cowrie shells. The beaded strip covering the mouth (fig. 260) is symbolic of secrecy among the young Bapende initiates.

Beads of metal, ivory, bone, shells, nuts, seeds, and glass are also used to decorate royal objects associated with the ceremonies of the court: crowns, robes, drums, thrones, and fetish objects. Most tribal designs, usually geometric motifs of triangles and interlacing diamond patterns, have symbolic importance. The various Bantu groups of South Africa are most skillful in fashioning geometric motifs which usually carry a message or state a proverb. The people of the Venda tribe, for instance, believe very strongly in ancestor worship, and the symbol of this tradition is the ancestor bead to which much reverence is attached. The Xhosa people of South Africa produce what is probably the most beautiful beadwork, and beads are an important part of their dress.

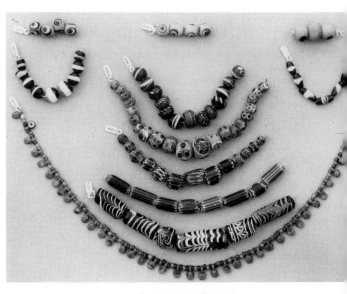

255. *Ancient beads of Egypt*

174

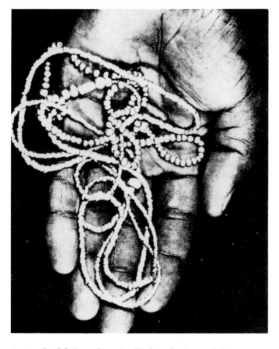

256. Gold "trade wind" beads found in an ex-cavation in Rhodesia dating to the third and fourth centuries A.D.

257. Aggrey beads of Ghana

258. Ndebele beaded bottles from Pretoria (South Africa)

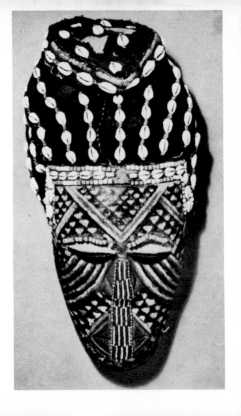

259. *Above: A woman's beaded apron decorated with Ndebele symbolic designs (South Africa)*

260. *Above right: A Bakuba initiation mask of the Babende Society (Central Zaïre); the band of beads over the mouth symbolizes the oath of secrecy*

261. *Below left: A Bushongo mask called Mashamboy (Zaïre); these masks belong to chiefs and represent clan heroes. They are worn today by professional dancers for entertainment, though the wearers must be men of royal ancestry.*

262. *Below right: A Yoruba beaded crown (Nigeria)*

263. A chief of Cameroon on his beaded throne

264. A newly married Xhosa couple wearing their beaded finery (South Africa)

265. These beaded blanket pins from South Africa carry significant love messages

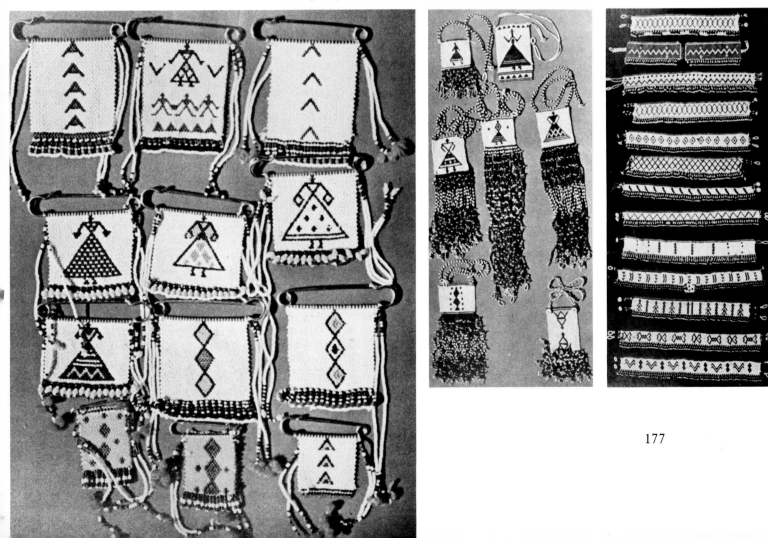

266. *Above: Beaded Xhosa girls grinding corn*

267. *Left: Beaded decorations are an important part of the Kikuyu dress (Kenya)*

268. *A beaded necklace from Salisbury, Rhodesia*

269. Below: *A Zulu headdress and ornate collar of beads (South Africa)*

270. *Another Zulu beaded costume*

II. WALL DECORATION

In decorating the walls of his home, the African artist generally works free-hand, spontaneously following his creative inspiration, as he did in the rock paintings of prehistoric times. In many areas it is customary to decorate both the interior and exterior walls of the home; beautiful outer wall designs are to be found among the Hima of Uganda, the Zande in Zaïre, and the Lunda of Angola. Much of the finest painting is reserved for royal residences and temples, as in Dahomey where reliefs built of clay and set into the walls form the exterior decoration on the dwelling of the chiefs (fig. 274). On many of these buildings, the relief panels form a kind of frieze and are painted in bright colors, with similar motifs carved on the wooden doors. The Hausa of Niger engrave or cast in high relief their clay facades with verses from the Koran, intricately designed to match surrounding geometric forms.

In most regions the geometric forms are made by the women, while the men borrow motifs from traditional beliefs and legends. Often brushes are used, but sometimes feathers or sticks are shaped to apply color, and some artists make skillful use of their fingers. The colors vary widely from region to region: red is made from the natural ochres, black from burned animal matter and charcoal, blue from the manufactured blueing introduced by Europeans, and white from kaolin or dried animal dung.

The patterns used on the interior walls of Hima huts are particularly rich in variety. These are formed by the application of black and white mud to the wall, a task performed by the old women of the tribe. According to tradition, it is in a decorated hut in the home village of her parents that a daughter is given by her father to the clan of her bridegroom, though there seems to be no rule deciding whether the patterns should be renewed after the ceremony or allowed to crumble away.

271. A doorway in Bamako, Sudan

272. Opposite above: Motifs for wall decoration and a Moorish doorway in Mauritania

273. Below: *A decorated house in Dahomey*

274. *Above: Bas-reliefs on the royal palace of Abomey in Dahomey*
275. *Below: Reliefs on a Dahomeyan wall representing artists' tools*

276. *The decorations on the walls of this Hausa dwelling in Nigeria were used only on interior walls until the end of the nineteenth century*

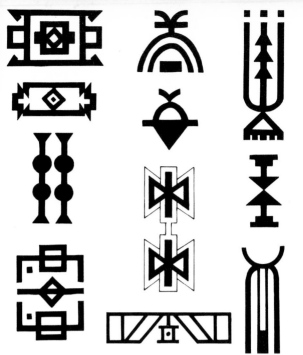

277. Opposite below: A contemporary Nubian house displays symbols and emblems dating back to Pharaonic times

278. Above left: Ndebele wall designs (South Africa)

279. Above right: A mural on a house in the village of Ekibondo(Zaïre)

280. Right: A Ghana house as recorded by T. E. Bowditch in 1849

281. A Bushongo house covered with decorated matting (Zaïre)

183

282. *An Ekibondo craftsman at work (Zaïre)*

283. *Wall decoration in Angola*

284. *Decorated houses of the Musgu, who live on the southern shore of Lake Chad*

285. *A decorated clay hut (Zambia)*

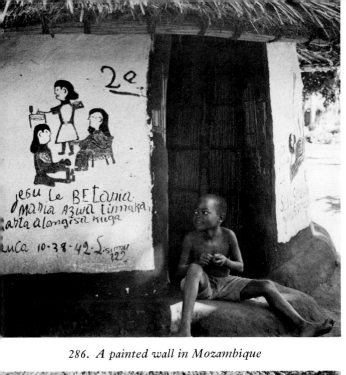

286. *A painted wall in Mozambique*

287. *House decoration in Tanzania*

288. *A typical Arab door in East Africa (Tanzania)*

289. *Designs for huts of the Hima tribe (Uganda)*

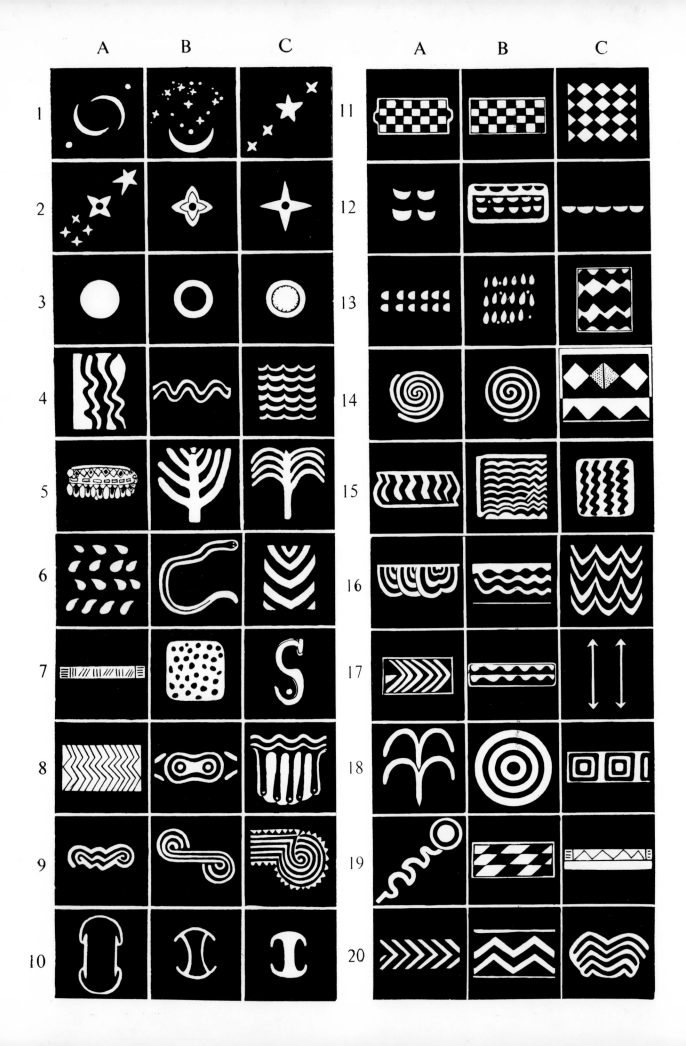

1. A. *okwezi n'enganzi n'akaringa*, the moon, the favorite (the planet Venus) and *Akaringa*, (the name of a particular star).

   B. *okwezi n'akakaaga*, the moon and the Pleiades.

   C. *basatu nibatunga njeru*, three people steal a white cow.
   Representing a star picture, probably the belt of Orion or Auriga.

2. A. *kyabahembezi eimutsya abakami*, *kyabahembezi* (the name of a particular star) awakens the people to milk the cows.

   B. *enganzi y'okwezi*, the favorite of the moon.
   Representing the planet Venus.

   C. *enyonyozi*, a star, *or*
   Rumaranku, literally that which finishes the fire wood.
   Rumaranku refers to a particular star.

3. A. *ekizoora*, the full moon, *or*
   eizooba, the sun.

   B. *eizooba kyakira*, an eclipse, literally: the sun is dark, *or*
   ekizooba kyeshereka, the sun hides, *or*
   ekikaari ky'okwezi, the halo of the moon, literally: the enclosure of the moon.

   C. *ekikaari ky'eizooba*, the halo of the sun, literally: the enclosure of the sun.

4. A. *ebingonzi by'amaizi*, waves of water.

   B. *omugyera*, brook.

   C. *ebigaaga*, water plants (papyrus?).

5. A. *ebishaka by'omu irungu*, bushes in the desert.
   Bushes like these were once seen by warriors as they passed through desert country.

   B. *enkukuuru*, euphorbia.

   C. *omukindo*, palm tree.

6. A. *amababi*, leaves.

   B. *enjoka n'omuhanda gwayo*, the snake and its trail.
   The cobra is the sacred animal of the royal clan *Bahinda*.

   C. *akabunu k'enturegye*, the buttocks of a zebra.

7. A. *akababa k'enyangye*, wing of an egret.

   B. *ekicweka ky'akanyana ka bugondo*, a part of a spotted calf.

   C. *omuranga gw'ente*, mark on a cow.
   Brand marks are used to indicate ownership.

8. A. *kanyarara*, wet from rain.
   Literally: little stripes (?)
   Reference is made to rivulets of water running off the fur of a cow, *or*
   enkokora z'abahundami, elbows of thin people.

   B. *amaisho g'abanyoro*, the eyes of the lords.
   This refers to the legendary *Bacwezi*. Note that *abanyoro* is not a Lunyankole word.

   C. *ekisingo ky'enshoni*, veil of modesty.
   A veil made of strands of beads is worn to conceal the face of a woman who worships the *Bacwezi* and who is possessed by a spirit (*embandwa*). Her eyes must not be seen in this condition.

9. A. *enteko y'abatabaazi*, a crowd of warriors.
   Patterns placed on the upper arm of a man. They represent the formation of men on a military expedition finding new homes.

   B. another version of the above.

   C. another version of the above.

10. A. *enanga y'abahima*, the trough zither of the Hima, *or*
    nyarushara, derived from *enshara*, a cow with drooping horns.

    The reference is to the horns carved at both ends of the zither.

    B. another version of the above.

    C. another version of the above.

11. A. *ekishoro*, board for the *mweso* game.

    B. *enkiri*, rock.
    The reference is to depressions in the surface of a rock, for the *mweso* game (?).

    C. *muharimu*, handkerchief.
    The kind of cloth first brought to Ankole by Arab traders. From Arabic *maharimu*.

12. A. *amajugo*, pellet bells.

    B. another version of the above.

    C. another version of the above.

13. A. *ebirezi by'omu maraka*, beads for the neck.

    B. *obwana bw'ensimbi*, small cowrie shells.

    C. *ebishonga by'ekisingo*, triangular patterns of a veil. Cf. 8.C. above.

14. A. *enshunju z'abahimakazi*, hair styles of Hima women.

    B. *enshunju z'akakanga*, hair styles known as *akakanga*.

    C. *ebishonga by'omu mitwe y'abahima*, pointed hair styles of Hima men.

15. A. *engondo z'abahima*, patterns used by Hima men. These patterns are worn on the arm.

    B. *eminyaafu*, switch.
    Used for driving cattle. Roscoe (1923) describes it as "an emblem of peace and happiness."

    C. *engondo*, patterns.
    Marked on men's arms. The patterns are put on when the rains break and the herds return from the search for water.

16. A. *omwenombo*, patterns.
    The patterns are marked on the chest of a child.

    B. *engondo*, patterns.
    Marked on the body.

    C. *ebinyamahembe*, weals. Literally: things with horns.

17. A. *akajengyeio*, small wooden container for needles.

    B. *omutana*, wooden quiver.

    C. *emyambi*, arrows.

18. A. *emihoro*, billhooks.
    The pattern is comparable to the shape of the *mpiima* of the Kabaka.

    B. *embazi z'enju*, rings of the roof of a hut.

    C. *ebitebe*, stools, *or*
    endorero, spy holes.

19. A. *emihanda etaaha Rukoma*, tracks leading to the *Rukoma*.
    The pattern illustrates the tabu that forbids anyone approaching the Coronation Rukoma (i.e. the royal enclosure?) to look into the gate.

    B. *ebishonga*, triangular patterns. Cf. 13.C. and 14.C

    C. *kanyanya*, little sister.
    No explanation for the name could be given.

20. A. another version of the above.

    B. another version of the above.

    C. Vernacular name and meaning unknown.

A READING LIST

Antuban, Kofi. *Ghana's Heritage of Culture*. Leipzig, 1963.

Bascom, William. *The Sociological Role of the Yoruba Cult Group*. American Anthropological Association, 1943.

Bascom, William R., and M. Herskovitz (eds.). *Continuity and Change in African Cultures*. Chicago, 1959.

Beier, Ulli. *Contemporary Art in Africa*. Praeger, 1968.

Beyer, Harry K. *Africa South of the Sahara*. New York, 1969.

Biobaku, Saburi O. *Ogboni, the Egba Senate*. Lagos, 1949.

Baos, Franz. *Primitive Art*. New York, 1965.

Boateng, E. A. *A Geography of Ghana*. London, 1959.

Bohannan, Paul. *Artist and Critic in an African Society*. London, 1961.

Brentjes, Burchard. *African Rock Art*. London, 1969.

Breuil, Henri. *Four Hundred Centuries of Cave Art*. Baden-Baden, 1953.

Briggs, L. C. *Tribes of the Sahara*. Princeton, 1960.

Brown, Leslie. *Africa, A Natural History*. New York, 1960.

Broster, Joan A. *Red Blanket Valley*. Johannesburg, 1967.

Buxton, David. *Travels in Ethiopia*. London, 1949.

Christensen. E. O. *Primitive Art*. New York, 1955.

Crowder, Michael. *A Short History of Nigeria*. New York, 1966.

Davidson, Basil. *Old Africa Rediscovered*. London, 1959.

_____. *The African Past: Chronicles from Antiquity to Modern Times*. London, 1965.

_____. *Africa: History of a Continent*. New York, 1966.

_____. *Saharan Painting*. New Statesman, 1958.

Douglas, Calvin. *African Art*. New York, 1969.

Eicher, Joanne B. *African Dress*. East Lansing, Michigan, 1969.

Fagg, William. *Nigerian Images*. New York, 1966.

Fraser, Douglas. *Primitive Art*. London, 1963.

Frobenius, Leo. *The Voice of Africa* (2 vols.). London, 1913.

_____. *Kulturgeschichte Afrikas*. Zurich, 1933.

Fuchs, Peter. *The Land of the Veiled Men*. Paris, 1947.

Gardi, René. *African Crafts and Craftsmen*. New York, 1969.

Gibbs, J. L. *Peoples of Africa*. New York, 1965.

Goldwater, Robert. *Traditional Art of the African Nations*. Museum of Primitive Art. New York, 1961.

Greenberg, J. H. *The Languages of Africa*. Bloomington Research Center in Anthropology, 1963.

Harrison, Church R. J. *West Africa: A Study of the Environment and Man's Use of It*. London, 1967.

Horton, Robin. *Kalabari Sculpture*. Lagos, 1965.

Huxley, Elspeth. *A New Earth*. New York, 1960.

Kay, G. *A Social Geography of Zambia*. London, 1960.

Kiewe, Heinz E. *Ancient Berber Tapestries and Rugs, Art Needlework Industries*.

_____. *Ancient Moroccan Embroideries*. Oxford, 1952.

_____. *Africa: Make Them Craftsmen*. Oxford, 1969.

Kitchen, Helen. *A Handbook of African Affairs*. New York, 1964.

Krueger, C. *Sahara*. New York, 1972.

Kyrematen, A. A. Y. *Panoply of Ghana*. London, 1964.

Latouche, John T., and Andre Cauvin. *Congo*. London, 1945.

Legum, Colin. *African Handbook*. New York, 1967.

Leiris, Michael, and Jaqueline Delange. *African Art*. London, 1968.

Lewis, I. (ed). *Islam in Tropical Africa*. London, 1968.

Leuzinger, Elsy. *Africa, The Art of the Negro Peoples*. New York, 1960.

Light, Richard U. *Focus on Africa.* American Geographic Society, 1941.

Locke, Alain, *Negro Art, Past and Present.* Washington, D. C., 1936.

Lommel, Andreas. *Prehistoric and Primitive Man.* New York, 1966.

Meyerowitz. Eva L. R. "The Shango Temple at Ibadan." *Man,* XLVII, p. 92.

Middleton, John, and E. H. Winter. *Witchcraft and Sorcery in East Africa.* New York, 1963.

Murdock, G. P. *Africa: Its People and Their Culture History.* New York, 1959.

National Geographic Society. *The River Nile.* Washington, D.C., 1966.

_____. *Vanishing Peoples of the Earth.* Washington, D.C., 1960.

Nida, Eugene. *Introducing Animism.* New York, 1959.

Ottenberg, Simon and Phoebe (eds.). *Cultures and Societies in Africa.* New York, 1960.

Pankhurst, S. *Ethiopia: A Cultural History.* London, 1959.

Parrinder, E. G. *Religion in an African City.* Oxford, 1953.

Plass, Margaret Webster. *The Webster Plass Collection of African Art.* London, 1953.

_____. *African Miniatures.* New York, 1967.

_____. *Metal Casting on the Guinea Coast.* London, 1957.

Plumer, Cheryl. *African Textiles.* East Lansing, Michigan, 1969.

Porter, James A. *The Appreciation of African Negro Art.* Washington, D.C., 1953.

Rattray, R. S. *Religion and Art in Ashanti.* London, 1959.

Redfield, Herskovits, and Ekholm. *Aspects of Primitive Art.* New York, 1959.

Schultess, Emil. *Africa.* New York, 1958.

Segy, Ladislas. *African Sculpture Speaks.* New York, 1952.

_____. *The Significance of African Art.* Atlanta, 1951.

_____. *Circle-dot Symbolic Signs on African Ivory Carvings.* Zaïre, 1953.

Sekintu, Charles. *Wall Patterns in Hima Huts.* Kampala, 1959.

Seligman, C. G. *Races of Africa.* New York, 1965.

_____. *Egypt and Negro Africa.* London, 1934.

Shinnie, Peter. *Meroe: A Civilization of the Sudan.* New York, 1966.

Smith, E. *African Symbolism.* Royal Anthropological Institute, London, 1952.

Snowden, F. M. *Blacks in Antiquity.* Cambridge, 1969.

Stapleton, G. B. *The Wealth of Nigeria.* London, 1967.

Stowe, William, and D. Bleek. *Rock Paintings in South Africa.* London, 1930.

Swithenbank, Michael. *Ashanti Fetish Houses.* Accra, 1965.

Taylor and Webb. *Customs of the Hausas.* Oxford, 1932.

Thompson, Robert F. *Testaments of Treasury: The 19th Century Legacy of Yoruba Culture.* New Haven, 1964.

Thompson, V., and R. Adloff. *The Malagasy Republic, Madagascar Today.* Stanford, 1965.

Trowell, Margaret. *African Design.* New York, 1965.

Tufuo, J. W., and E. E. Donkor, *The Ashantis of Ghana.* Accra, 1969.

Tyrrell, Barbara. *Tribal Peoples of Southern Africa.* Capetown, 1969.

Ullendorf, Edward. *The Ethiopians, an Introduction to Country and People.* London, 1965.

Wassing, René S. *African Art.* New York, 1968.

Willard, J. *The Great Sahara.* London, 1964.

Willett, Frank. *African Art.* New York, 1969.

Wingert, Paul S. *The Sculpture of Negro Africa.* New York, 1950.

AFRICAN STUDIES CENTERS

The following are among the most important African studies centers in the United States:

Africa Collection, Hoover Institution
Stanford University, Stanford, California

African Department
Northwestern University, Evanston, Illinois

African Collection
Yale University, New Haven, Connecticut

African Studies Center
Boston University, Boston, Massachusetts

Committee on African Studies
University of Chicago, Chicago, Illinois

African Studies Center
University of California, Los Angeles, California

East African Studies Program
Syracuse University, Syracuse, New York

Important centers in other countries:

Institute of Commonwealth Studies
University of London

Institute of Commonwealth Studies
University of Oxford

Centre of African Studies
University of Edinburgh

African Studies Centre
University of Cambridge

Committee on African Studies in Canada
University of Alberta

Scandinavian Institute of African Studies
University of Uppsala

PHOTO CREDITS

All photographs and drawings not credited below are by the author.

American Museum of Natural History, New York: 48
From Heinrich Barth, *Travels and Discoveries in North and Central Africa*, London, 1849: 85, 115, 158
From T. E. Bowditch, *Mission from Cape Coast Castle to Ashantee*, London, 1819: 280
British Museum, London: 163, 193, 226, 255
Joan A. Broster: 264, 265
R. Cte. de la Burde: 171, 172, 186
André Cauvin: 153
John Desmond Clark: 214
Cooper-Hewitt Museum, New York: 82, 83, 86, 87
Lewis Cotlow: 60
Cultural Service, Mali: 50
Dominique Darbois, Paris: 120, 225
E. H. Duckworth: 276
Eliot Elisofon: 261
Brian Fagan: 256
Folk Textile Collection, Heinz Edgar Kiewe, Oxford, England: 70, 71, 72, 73, 89, 102, 259
French Embassy Press and Information Division: 11, 12, 26, 51, 53, 55, 57, 58, 59, 67, 68, 100, 107, 111, 116, 117, 119, 125, 126, 127, 130, 139, 141, 147, 154, 155, 156, 157, 160, 178, 180, 181, 190, 223, 230, 244, 263, 271, 272, 273, 274, 275, 282
Friendship Textile Mills, Dar es Salaam: 65
Jean Gabus: 108, 109
René Gardi: 215
Ghana National Museum, Accra: 168, 169, 170, 194, 200, 208
L'Institut Fondamental d'Afrique Noire: 182
Metropolitan Museum of Art, New York: 225
Musée de l'Homme, Paris: 7, 103
Musée Royal de l'Afrique Centrale: 105, 143, 191
National Geographic Society: 34, 35
National Museum, Washington, D.C.: 84
Nigeria Museum, Lagos: 213, 247
Pretoria Department of Information: 56
Oscar Rampone: 234
R. S. Rattray, *Religion and Art in Ashanti*, London, 1959: 74
Barbara Rubin: 218, 219, 221
Satour: 9, 10, 36, 37, 40, 41, 136, 137, 232, 241, 258, 267, 269
Gasset de Saint-Saveur, *Civil Costumes of Today of All Known Peoples*, 1784–1787, Paris: 25
Sekintu, *Wall Patterns in Hima Huts*, Kampala, 1959: 290
Tanzania Information Services: 287
Robert Farris Thompson, Yale University: 262
Tunisian Embassy: 44, 70, 183, 184, 185, 249
Drawings after the style of Barbara Tyrrell as published in *Tribal Peoples of South Africa* by Books of Africa Ltd., Capetown, 1969: endpapers, 135, 141, 239, 270
Uganda Museum, Kampala: 289
University Museum, Philadelphia: 162
United Nations: 30, 80, 104, 144, 161, 177, 207, 216, 233, 238, 245, 251